CAMBRIDGE LIBRARY COLLECTION

Books of enduring scholarly value

Maritime Exploration

This series includes accounts, by eye-witnesses and contemporaries, of voyages by Europeans to the Americas, Asia, Australasia and the Pacific during the colonial period. Driven by the military and commercial interests of powers including Britain, France and the Netherlands, particularly the East India Companies, these expeditions brought back a wealth of information on climate, natural resources, topography, and distant civilisations. Their detailed observations provide fascinating historical data for climatologists, ecologists and anthropologists, and the accounts of the mariners' experiences on their long and dangerous voyages are full of human interest.

A Journal of a Voyage Round the World, in His Majesty's Ship *Endeavour*

This slim volume, published anonymously in 1771 within months of the *Endeavour*'s return from Captain Cook's first voyage, predates Hawkesworth's publication of Cook's own journal in his *Voyages* (1773, also reissued). It has been attributed variously to two of the ship's petty officers (Orton and Perry); Sydney Parkinson, draughtsman; his employer Joseph Banks; or the Swedish botanist Solander. The story moves rapidly, with well-chosen detail: mines that 'destroy two thousand slaves yearly', or the brown granite of a communal laundry. The author describes marine animals, Tahitian and New Zealand society, and foodstuffs including a 'large milky farinaceous fruit, which when baked resembles bread' – the breadfruit that Joseph Banks later decided to introduce to the Caribbean, leading to the ill-fated *Bounty* voyage (Bligh's account of which is also reissued). The author reports making 'considerable progress in learning the language of the country', and concludes with a short list of Tahitian words.

Cambridge University Press has long been a pioneer in the reissuing of out-of-print titles from its own backlist, producing digital reprints of books that are still sought after by scholars and students but could not be reprinted economically using traditional technology. The Cambridge Library Collection extends this activity to a wider range of books which are still of importance to researchers and professionals, either for the source material they contain, or as landmarks in the history of their academic discipline.

Drawing from the world-renowned collections in the Cambridge University Library and other partner libraries, and guided by the advice of experts in each subject area, Cambridge University Press is using state-of-the-art scanning machines in its own Printing House to capture the content of each book selected for inclusion. The files are processed to give a consistently clear, crisp image, and the books finished to the high quality standard for which the Press is recognised around the world. The latest print-on-demand technology ensures that the books will remain available indefinitely, and that orders for single or multiple copies can quickly be supplied.

The Cambridge Library Collection brings back to life books of enduring scholarly value (including out-of-copyright works originally issued by other publishers) across a wide range of disciplines in the humanities and social sciences and in science and technology.

A Journal of a Voyage Round the World,

in His Majesty's Ship *Endeavour*

In the Years 1768, 1769, 1770, and 1771;
Undertaken in Pursuit of Natural Knowledge,
at the Desire of the Royal Society

ANONYMOUS

CAMBRIDGE
UNIVERSITY PRESS

CAMBRIDGE
UNIVERSITY PRESS

University Printing House, Cambridge, CB2 8BS, United Kingdom

Cambridge University Press is part of the University of Cambridge.

It furthers the University's mission by disseminating knowledge in the pursuit of
education, learning and research at the highest international levels of excellence.

www.cambridge.org
Information on this title: www.cambridge.org/9781108082600

This edition first published 1771
This digitally printed version 2015

ISBN 978-1-108-08260-0 Paperback

A

JOURNAL

OF A

VOYAGE round the WORLD,

In His Majefty's Ship ENDEAVOUR,

In the Years 1768, 1769, 1770, and 1771;

Undertaken in Purfuit of NATURAL KNOWLEDGE, at the Defire of the ROYAL SOCIETY:

CONTAINING

ALL the various OCCURRENCES of the VOYAGE,

WITH

DESCRIPTIONS of feveral new difcovered Countries in the SOUTHERN HEMISPHERE; and Accounts of their Soil and Productions; and of many Singularities in the Structure, Apparel, Cuftoms, Manners, Policy, Manufactures, &c. of their Inhabitants.

To which is added,

A Concife VOCABULARY of the Language of OTAHITEE.

Ornari res ipfa negat, contenta doceri.   HOR.

LONDON,

Printed for T. BECKET and P. A. DE HONDT, in the Strand.

MDCCLXXI.

A

J O U R N A L

O F A

VOYAGE round the WORLD.

IN the beginning of the year 1768, the Britifh ambaffador at Madrid applied to the court of Spain for the grant of a paffport to a fhip defigned for California, to obferve the tranfit of Venus, which was promifed, with a provifion that the aftronomer fhould be a member of the Romifh church, and an Italian gentleman was confequently engaged for the undertaking; but the paffport when demanded was refufed by the Spanifh miniftry, who alledged that it was repugnant to the policy of government to admit foreigners into their American ports, unlefs driven there by neceffity; but efpecially thofe who by their profeffion would be fitted to make fuch obfervations as might facilitate the approaches and defcents of their enemies at any future war with Great Britain.

B   It

It was then determined to difpatch the Italian gentleman to Hudfon's Bay, and a fhip of four hundred tons burthen was purchafed for the voyage by order of the government. This fhip was named the Endeavour, and, according to the original plan, was to have been navigated by a mafter, a fecond mafter, a mate, two mid fhip men, and thirty feamen, who were engaged for the fervice, and orders were at the fame time iffued from the navy-office to equip her for the undertaking; and early in the month of May warrants were granted to the firft and fecond mafters, but recalled the following day, the plan of her voyage having been altered. But on the 27th of the fame month the fhip was again put in commiffion, and her compliment augmented to feventy men; an application was likewife made for a number of marines, but without fuccefs.

On the 21ft of July fhe fell down to Greenwich, and the next morning to the Galleons, where we received on board fix guns, being four-pounders, together with twelve fwivels, and gunner's ftores, &c. On the evening of the 30th we anchored at Gravefend, and the next morning proceeded towards the Downs, where we arrived on the 3d of Auguft, and on the fame day failed for Plymouth, where we came to anchor on the 14th, and

and were ordered to receive on board twelve marines,
and three additional feamen; which, with Mr. Green
the obferver, and his fervant, together with Mr. Banks
and Dr. Solander, and their attendants, who were confidered as fupernumeraries, encreafed our number to
ninety-fix fouls. We likewife received four additional
carriage-guns, and, having made feveral beneficial alter-
ations, were on the 20th of the fame month ready for
fea, but the wind blowing frefh at S. W. we were detained until the 25th, when it changing to N. N. W. we
put to fea at four o'clock in the afternoon. The wind
however foon became and continued fouth-wefterly until the 2d of September, when it changed to the northward; and at half paft five in the morning we difcovered
the land, bearing S. S. W. and at ten we diftinguifhed Cape
Ortugal, bearing S. E. by E. half E. and diftant feven
leagues. The winds were frefh but variable until the
4th, when at eight o'clock, A. M. we difcovered Cape
Finifterre, bearing S. W. by S. at ten leagues diftance.

From this time nothing remarkable occurred until the
12th, when at fix in the morning we faw Puerto Santo
at N. W. half N. and about nine leagues diftant; and
at feven we difcovered the ifland of Madeira at W. by N.
the Deferters appearing at the fame time W. by S. half

　　S. At

S. At eight the fame evening the fhip came to anchor with her beft bower in twenty-two fathom water. At five the next morning we weighed anchor to approach nearer the fhore, but the wind and tide being unfavourable, drove us farther diftant, and foon after we received two fhots from the Loo Fort, the commandant imagining it was our intention to depart from the ifland without making the ufual reports; and by this tranfaction he forfeited the compliment of a falute, ufually paid by foreign fhips of war to all fortifications. At length however we anchored again in fifteen fathom water; and the Britifh conful foon after waited on the governor to complain of the indignity we had received, for which an apology was made, and the conful was affured that the officer who had mifbehaved fhould afk pardon of Captain Cooke if he required it, but this was declined.

This town of Fonchial is the capital of the ifland, and gives name to the bay within which it is fituated. It is defended by a wall, and four or five baftions towards the bay, and has two gates. Its ftreets are narrow and ill-paved, but the houfes are high. The inhabitants are computed to be feven or eight thoufand in number, but among thefe there are but few gentlemen who are not

in

in trade, the greater part being fhop-keepers, who vend imported goods. The town contains two hofpitals, one of which is appropriated for Lepers, and the other for the general reception of the inferior people, who want either medical or chirurgical affiftance. It likewife contains a large Francifcan college, and a fpacious cathedral, but its churches in general are very inelegant. Here are likewife two convents, one of which I vifited feveral times, the abbefs behaving with great complaifance, and appearing to be the moft a-greeable of the fifterhood, among which I did not ob-ferve one who could pretend to more than a very mo-derate fhare of beauty. Mr. Banks and Dr. Solander likewife made them a vifit, and were afked many lu-dicrous queftions, as, When it would thunder and rain? Where they might find a fpring of frefh water within the walls of their convent? and others equally pregnant with credulous fimplicity; for they had conceived an opinion that thefe gentlemen were poffeffed of fome-thing like magical or fupernatural knowledge.

Here is alfo a Britifh factory, which confifts of a con-ful, vice-conful, and twenty-two merchants, from which number ten are felected, and four of thefe are annually chofen by rotation, to direct the bufinefs of the factory

in

in conjunction with the conful; they all however pay
equal fhares of the taxes impofed for defraying the ex-
pences of the factory, of which the greateft part is in-
curred in maintaining an hofpital, with its phyfician,
furgeon, &c. To the eaftward of Fonchial is a fmaller
town, called Santa Cruz; thefe two are the only towns
on the ifland.

The governor, whofe falary and perquifites amount
to near eleven hundred pounds fterling per annnm, re-
fides at his feat about half a mile diftant from Fonchial;
there is however a caftle for his refidence in town, which
is defended by feveral cannon towards the bay, and is
feparated by a high wall from the town itfelf.

An Officer conftantly attends at Fonchial to receive
the compliments of Foreigners in the governor's behalf,
who declines them perfonally.

On our firft arrival the Britifh conful folicited permiffion for Mr. Banks, Dr. Solander, and their attendants to vifit the country; but the governor would permit no more than two of them to go abroad at a time;
until afterwards, being more particularly informed of
their errand, he gave them full liberty to purfue their
                                        refearches

researches at pleasure, and paid them a visit in person, and was entertained with electrical and other philosophical experiments.

The island of Madeira was discovered in the year 1419, by the Portuguese fleet under the command of John Gonzales Zareo Tristan Vaz & Perello, who was sent out to attempt the passage of Cape Bajador the year after the discovery of the island of Puerto Santo.

It is situated in latitude 32° 33′ 33″, and longitude 16° 49′ 45″ West from London; the variation by several observations was found to have decreased westerly 15° 30′, the dipping-needle being 77° 18′. The best anchoring ground is near the Loo Castle, in twenty, twenty-five, or thirty fathom, the East side of the bay being hard, rocky ground. The island is computed to contain sixty thousand inhabitants; its longest extent is between N.E. and S.W. It rises very high, and terminates in a peak, called Pico Rucco, which is five thousand and sixty-eight feet in height. The land rises by very unequal elevations from the sea, and forms a ridge which is frequently interrupted by chasms of unequal depths; these extend almost the whole length of the island. This inequality of the surface of the ground has made it ne-

ceffary

ceffary to extend the roads in ferpentine windings, to avoid thofe deep gullies which have formed themfelves in almoft every part, of which the moft confiderable run in pretty ftrait directions towards the fea, and are commonly charged with large ftreams of water; but thefe in approaching the fea are gradually diminifhed by the peafants, who are allowed to draw off certain quantities of water by fmall ditches, according to the fize of their vineyards, which are to be watered thereby.

The ifland produces fix kinds of grapes, viz. the Malmfey, two black, and three white kinds. It is the fkin of the black grapes that tinges the wines of Madeira, the juice itfelf being white; hence the difference of colour in thefe wines arifes from the different proportions in which the black and white grapes arc mixed. It is commonly reported that no diftilled fpirit is added to thefe wines, but I have been well affured of the contrary, and have feen the fpirit ufed for that purpofe. The beft Madeira is fold at twenty-fix pounds per pipe; the worft kind, which is made on the North fide, is fold for thirteen pounds; this is the contract wine, and is the fame which is drank by the common people. The Madeira imported into Great Britain is fold at twenty-three pounds per pipe; there are two inferior forts

which

which bear the name of Madeira, one of which is fold at eighteen, and the other at fixteen pounds. All thefe wines improve greatly by fea voyages; and of this the inhabitants are fo well convinced, that almoft all the wines defigned for their own confumption are fent feveral times to fea.

The Malmfey is a moft excellent wine, and is fold at forty pounds per pipe. It is generally computed by the merchants, that the quantity of wine produced in Madeira is between thirty and thirty-five thoufand pipes annually, of which ten thoufand are exported to Great Britain and her colonies.

Six fhips are permitted to fail from hence to Brafil every year loaded with wine. I faw no carriages during our ftay at Madeira, but was told of a fedan kept by an Englifh gentleman. We found the longitude of Puerto Santo by obfervation, 16° 56′ W. and its latitude 33° 00′ N.

September 19. The wind changing to E. S. E. we weighed anchor and ftood to fea. The weather continuing favourable, on the 22d we faw the iflands of Salvages, S. S. W. half W. diftant eight miles; they are

C   two

two fmall uninhabited iflands, fituated between Madeira and the Canaries. The 23d we reached the trade-winds, then at N. E. and the fame day we difcovered the Peak of Teneriffe, the largeft of the Canary iflands, being forty-five miles in length. The Peak, according to Dr. Halley, is two miles and a quarter in height; but by Dr. Heberden it is computed at fifteen thoufand three hundred and ninety-five feet; in clear weather it may be feen thirty-feven leagues at fea. This ifland produces wine, fruits, and cattle; its chief town is called Laguna. September 24, we failed between the Grand Canaries and Teneriffe, the trade-wind blowing frefh with a thick haze. At this time we obferved many things rufting and moulding. On the 27th the wind and fea continuing favourable, we began to ferve the fhip's crew with wine and four krout. On the 28th feveral land birds were difcovered, of which we caught two, nearly refembling the yellow water-wagtail. The 29th, at eleven A. M. we faw the ifland of Bona Vifta, at N. 48° W. and diftant eleven miles. October 2d we perceived a current fetting E. S. E. and W. N. W. From this time nothing remarkable occured, until the 7th, when the winds became variable from South to Weft, with frequent fhowers of rain. This day we caught two fwallows and feveral marine animals.

animals. All our iron utenfils rufted very much, and every thing fufceptible of mould was covered with it; many of our feamen were likewife affected with bilious diforders. The wind continued variable until the 19th, when it became fouth-eafterly, and the 21ft we entered the S.E. trade. At this time we began to brew fweet wort for thofe who were affected with the fcurvy*. The wind continued favourable until the 4th of November, when at five in the afternoon the fun was in our zenith, notwithftanding it was colder by feveral degrees than it had been a few days before; the thermometer, which had been at 80°, having fell to 77°. The wind continued variable, with frequent fqualls, until the 7th, when at fix o'clock, P.M. we founded and reached bottom at thirty-two fathom, the ground confifting of coral-rock, fine fand, and broken fhells, At three o'clock the water deepened to thirty-eight fathoms, and at four to eighty fathoms; at fix we found no ground within one hundred fathom.

Tuefday the 8th, the winds continuing variable, at fix A.M. we difcovered the land bearing N.W. feven

---

* This remedy was firft propofed by Dr. Mackbride, who by many experiments found it fitted to fupply the want of frefh vegetables, by generating large quantities of fixed air, which is poffeffed of the moft antifcorbutic and antifeptic qualities.

or

or eight leagues diftant; we had again foundings between thirty-feven and forty eight fathoms, with coarfe
brown fand, and coral-rock. At ten o'clock we fpoke
with a fmall Portuguefe fifhing veffel, from which Mr.
Banks purchafed dolphin, bream, and other fifh, about
one hundred and fifty in number, which he gave to the
fhip's company. This veffel was manned with eleven
people, two of whom were whites, and the others negroes. She belonged to the captainfhip of Spirito
Santo; but her crew appeared very ignorant of the
coaft, for on our enquiring the diftance of Cape Frio
and of Cape Thomas, we found they did not know one
from the other.

Our interpreters were a Venetian and a Portuguefe,
who told us that the crew of the fifhing veffel declared
they had not feen a fhip within eight years: but this
I prefume was a miftake; as they fpoke fuch imper-
fect Englifh that we found it almoft impoffible to un-
ftand them. I have before mentioned that fix veffels
are annually fent from Madeira hither, befides the fhips
of war and merchantmen that arrive from Lifbon.
After parting from the fifhing veffel we ftood in towards the land, which appeared very high in three remarkable hills. From this until the 13th, we failed

along

along the coaft towards Ifle Frio, which is in latitude
23° 8′ S. and longitude 38° 30′ W.   North from Cape
Frio is a flat, extending a long way from the fhore,
which we fuppofed to be irregular, having varied out
foundings greatly between Cape Spirito Santo and Ifle
Frio.   In failing for Rio Janeiro it is neceffary to make
this ifland, from which the courfe to the harbour's
mouth by the compafs is Weft, and it is beft to fail
pretty near the fhore.

Without the harbour, on the ftarboard quarter, are
two iflands, of which the innermoft is very high and
conic; the other at one end has a prominence, which
appears like a third ifland.

When thefe iflands bore S. W. by W. at five miles
diftance, they appeared but as one; however as we advanced within the entrance they opened very diftinctly.
There is alfo an ifland juft without, a fugar-loaf, or
promontory on the main land, but it is not obferved in
coming from the northward.   Between the higheft of
thefe iflands and the fhore are three or four fmall rocky
iflands,

The

The promontory or fugar-loaf is called Monte de St. Juan, but the conical peak is Pointre de Sucre. This promontory ftands on a peninfula at the Weft fide of the river; the peninfula itfelf forms a large bay; and within the bite, without the fugar-loaf, is a fandy beach, which is fortified by a battery that has twenty-two embrafures, and is defigned to oppofe a landing on the peninfula, where there are feveral other batteries and a regular fort, called Forte de St. Juan, which if taken by an enemy would command the fortifications of Rock Ifland, fituated before it in the entrance of the river, and juft oppofite the fort of St. Cruz, on the other fide of the paffage. After landing on the peninfula, an army might eafily approach the town, which is itfelf quite defencelefs, by climbing over the ridge of hills, and defcending to the plain on which it is fituated.

Ilho de Lozio, or Rock Ifland, which lies before the promontory, has a very ftrong fortification of an hexagonal form; and oppofite thereto on the Eaft fhore is the fort of St. Cruz, which is efteemed the ftrongeft of all thofe that defend the river. We are told that there was a funken rock before this fort and that of Ilho de Lozio, which together command the entrance of the river which is about half a mile wide.

The

The fort of St. Cruz is furrounded by a deep wide ditch cut through a folid rock, which renders it diffi-cult of approach by land; but being fituated on a low point, it would be greatly expofed to the fire of fhips, and unable to withftand the attacks of a Britifh fleet.

Above the fort of St. Cruz are two batteries, one of fix guns, fituated on the main, and the other on a high ifland called Ilho de bon Voyage.

Farther up the river and on the Weft fide is another ifland, called Berghalion, on which is a battery with twenty feven embrafures, but I obferved that guns were not mounted in them all. The courfe up the river is N. N. W. Before the town there is an ifland called Ilhos dos Scobros, or Snake Ifland; this forms or covers the harbour, and is to be ftrongly fortified. From the South end of it there is a fhoal that extends obliquely towards the main, and the paffage into the harbour is round the North end.

Sunday the 13th, at eight A. M. we failed in towards the harbour of Rio Janeiro, in latitude 22° 56' South, and longitude 42° 45 Weft, having before difpatched a lieutenant and mate in our pinnace to the viceroy, to

procure

procure a pilot; but as the wind continued favourable, we failed onwards without waiting their return, and left the iflands in the entrance of the river at our right, at the fame time we obferved fignals from the different forts.

Monday the 14th, when ftanding into the harbour our pinnace returned with a military officer difpatched by the viceroy, who had detained our own lieutenant and mate; and as no pilot had been fent, we ftood forwards into the harbour, and came to anchor in five fathoms of water, near the North end of Snake's Ifland, and at about a quarter of a mile diftance from Ilho dos Ferreres or Pump Ifland. Soon after this we were vifited by a military colonel and two civil officers, who came on board from the cuftom-houfe-boat, and examined our fhip, enquired the number of our empty watercafks, and defired permiffion to infpect our log-book, which was granted. The colonel informed Mr. Banks and Dr. Solander that they had liberty to go afhore, but when he faw them preparing to do it, he advifed them to ftay until the next day. He likewife told us that the detention of our officers until after the examination of our fhip was a cuftomary precaution. Soon after receiving this information, Captain Cooke prepared to vifit

the

the viceroy, but was told he was then engaged, and would fee him the next morning. A refolution was however taken in council the fame day to grant us all neceffary fupplies, but to prohibit every one from coming on fhore; a prohibition which was very mortifying to us all, but efpecially to Mr. Banks and Dr. Solander, who had undertaken this voyage only in purfuit of natural knowledge.

It is to be obferved, that the lieutenant who had been firft fent to the viceroy for a pilot, was directed to evade any queftions that might be afked concerning our deftination or the object of our voyage; or at leaft to anfwer them with great referve, Captain Cooke judging that fuch queftions concerning a fhip of war would be impertinent. And as the lieutenant conducted himfelf agreeable to this direction, it is not improbable that his behaviour partly contributed to the reftraints that were impofed on us. We had indeed, whilft entering the river and harbour, publicly taken furveys of the country; and it was alfo reported that feveral gentlemen on board were men of uncommon erudition, who had been exprefsly fent abroad to make obfervations and difco veries. Thefe circumftances, together with fome commercial difagreements, which at that time were fup-

D

pofed to fubfift between Great Britain and Portugal, doubtlefs excited unfavourable fufpicions in the government of Rio Janiero, and occafioned the prohibition I have before mentioned, which Mr. Banks however occafionally found means to evade, by employing a failor to penetrate into the country by bribing the centinels, and there load himfelf with plants and fhrubs, collected indifcriminately, and afterwards convey them on board.

But, notwithftanding all the precautions taken by the viceroy, we obtained fufficient knowledge of Rio Janiero during our ftay there; partly from our own obfervations, and partly from the information of fome of its inhabitants of other nations. The navigation to its harbour is far from being difficult; fince, though unprovided with a pilot, we no where found lefs than fix fathoms of water, but a little above the fort of St. Cruz we obferved a ftrong eddy, that obliged us to keep nearer to the ftarboard fhore. The river itfelf forms a large bay above the town, which contains feveral iflands, from thence it extends north eafterly a great diftance into the country. The harbour itfelf is very capacious, having room for fixty or feventy fail of fhips; and it actually contained feveral of four hundred tons burthen.

The

The town of Rio Janiero is fituated on the Weft fide of the river, from which it extends itfelf about three quarters of a mile.   The ground on which it ftands is a level plain; it is defended on the North fide by a hill that extends from the river, leaving a fmall plain, which contains the fuburbs and the king's dock.   On the South fide is another hill, running towards the mountains which are behind the town.   Some of its ftreets run parallel from North to South, and are in-terfected by others at right angles. The principal ftreet is near an hundred feet in width, and extends from St. Benedict to the foot of Caftle-hill; the inferior are com-monly twenty or thirty feet wide.   The houfes ad-joining to the principal ftreet have three ftories, but in other places they are very irregular, though built after the fame manner as in Lifbon.   In the town are four convents; the firft is that of the Benedictines, fituated near its northern extremity; this ftructure affords an agreeable profpect, and contains an elegant chapel, which is ornamented with feveral valuable paintings. The fecond is that of the Carmelites, which forms the centre angle of the royal fquare, and fronts the har-bour; its church had fallen fome time before, but it is again rebuilding in a very elegant manner with fine free-ftone brought thither from Lifbon.   The third is

D 2

that

that of St. Anthony, fituated on the point of a hill on the South fide of the town; before this convent ftands a large bafon of brown granite, in the form of a parallelogram, which is employed in wafhing. The fourth is fituated at the eaftern extremity of the town, and was formerly the Jefuits convent, but is now converted into a military hofpital.

The viceroy's palace forms the right angle of the royal fquare: the palace, mint, ftables, goal, &c. compofe but one large building, which has two ftories, and is ninety feet from the water. In paffing through the palace, the firft entrance is to a large hall or guard-room, to which there is an afcent of three or four fteps. In the guard-room are ftationed the body guards who attend the viceroy, and are relieved every morning between eight and nine. Adjoining to the hall are the ftables, the prifon being in the back part of the building. Within the guard-room is a flight of ftairs for afcending to the upper ftory; this divides at a landing-place about half way, and forms two branches, one leading to the right, and the other to the left. The former enters a faloon, where there are two officers in conftant attendance; the viceroy's aid-du camp at the

fame

fame time waiting in an antichamber to receive meffages and deliver orders.

The left wing of the royal fquare is an irregular building, which confifts chiefly of fhops occupied by trading people. In the center of the fquare is a fountain fupplied with water from a fpring at the diftance of three miles, from which it is brought by an aqueduct. From this fountain both the fhipping and inhabitants are fupplied with water, the place being continually crowded with negroes of both fexes waiting to fill their jars. At every corner of the ftreets is an altar. The market-place extends from the North-Eaft end of the fquare along the fhore; and this fituation is very convenient for the fifhing boats, and thofe who bring vegetables, &c. from the other fide of the river to market. Negroes are almoft the only people employed in felling the different commodities expofed in the market, and they employ their leifure time in fpinning of cotton.

Without the Jefuits college on the fhore is a village called Neuftra Seignora del Gloria, which is joined to the town by a very few intervening houfes. Three or four hundred yards within the Jefuits convent ftands a very high caftle, but it is falling to decay.

The

The biſhops palace is about three hundred yards behind the Benedictine convent, and contiguous to it is a magazine of arms, furrounded by a rampart.

The gentry here keep their chaiſes, which are drawn by mules ; the ladies however uſe a ſedan chair, boarded before and behind, with curtains on each ſide, which is carried by two negroes, depending from a pole connected to the top of the chair by two iron rods coming from under its bottom, one on each ſide, and reſting at the top. The inhabitants likewiſe uſe hammocks or rajas, ſupported in the ſame manner, and furrounded with curtains.

In this town the apothecaries ſhops commonly ſerve the purpoſes of a coffee-houſe, people meeting in them to drink capillaire and play at back-gammon. The gentry when ſeen abroad are well dreſſed, though at home they are but looſely covered: the ſhopkeepers have commonly ſhort hair, and wear linen jackets with ſleeves. Beggars, who infeſt the ſtreets of moſt European cities, are not to be found in this: and as the genteeler proſtitutes here make there aſſignations at church, it is not uncommon for huſbands who are ſolicitous for the ſole enjoyment of their wives, to ſend

them

them to mafs at two or three o'clock in the morning; but the men of intrigue frequently avail themfelves of the opportunities which thofe early hours afford.

The climate of Rio Janiero is both agreeable and healthy, being free from many inconveniencies that are incident to other tropical countries. The air is but feldom immoderately hot, as the fea breeze conftantly begins to blow about ten o'clock in the morning, and continues until night, when it is generally fucceeded by a land wind, though this does not always happen. The feafons are divided into rainy and dry; though their ftationary periods have lately become very irregular and uncertain: indeed the rainy feafons had almoft entirely failed the four years preceding our arrival, at which time the rains had juft begun, and they fell in large quantities during our ftay: formerly the ftreets have been overflowed by the rain, and rendered impaffable except with canoes.

The adjacent country is mountainous, and chiefly covered with wood, but a fmall part of it appearing to be cultivated. The foil near the town is loofe and fandy, but farther from the river it is a fine black mould. It produces all the tropical fruits, fuch as

oranges,

oranges, lemons, limes, melons, mangoes, cocoa-nuts, &c. in great abundance, and without much cultivation; a circumftance which is very agreeable to the inhabitants, who are all indolent.

The mines, where they deftroy two thoufand flaves yearly, are at the diftance of about five days journey from the town. About twelve months before our arrival, the government had detected feveral jewellers in carrying on an illicit trade for diamonds with the flaves in the mines; and immediately after a law paffed, making it felony to work at the trade, or have any tools in poffeffion, the civil officers having indifcriminately feized on all that could be found.

There are feveral courts of juftice in town, at all of which the viceroy prefides; in criminal caufes the fentence is regulated by a majority of voices in the fupreme court. The viceroy has a council appointed from Europe by the king, to affift him in his private department, where he has two voices. The prefent viceroy is Antonio Rolim de Moura, Conde d'Azambuja; he is a little old man, and has enjoyed his prefent office about three years, having formerly been governor of Bahia for a long time.

The

The inhabitants of Rio Janiero maintain a whale-fishery, which supplies them with lamp-oil. They import their brandy from the Azores, their slaves and East India goods from their settlements in Africa, their wine from Madeira, and their European goods from Lisbon.

Thursday, December 8, 1768, having procured all necessary supplies, we left Rio Janiero, sailing along the coast to the southward, without any remarkable occurrence, until the 22d, when we discovered numerous birds of the Procillaria genus, being then in latitude 39° 37′ S. and longitude 49° 16 W. we were also frequently surrounded by great numbers of porpoises, of a singular species; the head having a remarkable convexity towards the mouth, from which the lower mandible appeared to protrude with a rounding chin. On the upper and back part of the head appeared a hole of about three inches diameter, through which the animal respires: on each side of the head appeared a white streak, extending backwards; and on the back was a large triangular white spot, its base being contiguous to the dorsal fin. Another of these spots was seen under the throat, and a third under the belly.

E

They

They are about fifteen feet in length, and of an aſh colour.

December 23d we obſerved an eclipſe of the moon; and about ſeven o'clock in the morning a ſmall white cloud appeared in the Weſt, from which a train of fire iſſued, extending itſelf weſterly: about two minutes after we heard two diſtinct loud exploſions immediately ſucceeding each other like cannon, after which the cloud ſoon diſappeared.

December 24, we caught a large loggerhead tortoiſe, weighing one hundred and fifty pounds. We likewiſe ſhot ſeveral birds, among which was an albetroſs, meaſuring between the tips of its wings nine feet and an inch; and from its beak to the tail, two feet one inch and an half. The thermometer at evening uſually ſtood at about 62°, and at mid-day between 66° and 69°. About this time we obſerved leſs appearance of ruſt and mould than formerly. The 27th we diſcovered ſeveral parcels of rock-weed. The 28th we had hard gales of wind at S. E.—S. and S. W. which obliged us to lie-to under our mainſail. The ſame day we had ſoundings between forty-ſix and fifty fathoms, with fine brown ſand; this was in 40° 50′ South latitude

tude, and 58° 16 Weſt longitude. The 29th the weather was moderate, and we founded in forty-ſix, forty-
nine, and forty-ſeven fathom, with fine grey ſand.
The 30th we had variable winds, with calms; our
foundings had not differed from thoſe of yeſterday.
We ſaw a ſea-lion. For ſeveral days about this time
we obſerved numerous ſwarms of butterflies, moths,
and beetles, flying round us. The 31ſt we had much
thunder, lightning, and rain: this and the three following days we ſaw ſeveral whales, and likewiſe ſeveral birds, about the ſize of a pigeon, with white bellies
and grey beaks.

January 4, 1769, we ſaw an appearance of land,
which we miſtook for Pepys iſland; but it diſappeared
on our ſtanding towards it. The air was cold and dry:
we founded in ſeventy-two fathoms, and found black
ſand and mud; and had frequent ſqualls about this
time, and obſerved great quantities of very long rock-
weed. The 6th we ſaw ſeveral penguins, and many
other birds. The 7th we had an exceſſive hard gale at
S. W. which compelled us to lie-to; being then in latitude 51° 25 S. and longitude 62° 44' W. we ſuppoſed
ourſelves abreaſt of Falkland-Iſlands; but their longitude
was ſo imperfectly known, that we were at a loſs to de-

E 2

termine

termine on which fide they were fituated.   The 8th we
founded in eighty fathoms, and found black brown
fand.   From feveral circumftances it was concluded
that we had paffed between Falkland Iflands and the
main land : the air was at this time very cold, but
healthy.   The 9th we faw feveral penguins and feals.
The 11th we difcovered Terra del Feugo; but having
contrary winds until the 15th, we endeavoured to anchor in the bay of Good Succefs, a little to the weftward
of the ftreights, that we might have the benefit of a
whole tide to carry us from the coaft; but in ftanding
towards it we found the foundings fo very unequal and
irregular, that we apprehended danger from the foul
nefs of the ground, and again ftood out to fea.   The
16th, having both wind and tide in our favour, we
failed into Port Maurice, and came to anchor.   This
bay is furrounded by very high land, well covered with
wood: it is fituated in latitude 54° 44 South, and longitude 66° 15 Weft, by obfervation: here, in a deferted
hut, we found feveral pieces of brown European broad-
cloth. The 17th, at ten A. M. we weighed anchor, and
turned into the bay of Good Succefs, where we anchored
at one in the afternoon, mooring our fhip in nine fathoms water, with the ftream anchor at N. W. and
immediately after went in fearch of a convenient place

to

to wood and water.   Captain Cooke, Mr. Banks, and
Dr. Solander likewife went afhore to meet fome Indians,
who appeared on a beach at the head of the bay, and
foon after brought three of them on board, cloathed
them with jackets, and gave them bread, jerked beef,
&c. part of which they eat, and carried the remainder
on fhore.   They refufed to drink rum or brandy, after
tafting them, intimating by figns that it burnt their
throats.   This circumftance may perhaps corroborate
the opinion of thofe who think water the natural drink
of mankind, as of all other animals.   One of thefe Indians made feveral long and loud fpeeches, though no
part of either was intelligible to any of us.   Another
of them ftole the covering of a globe, which he con-
cealed under his fkin garment, and carried on fhore,
where he took it out in the prefence of thofe from
whom he had ftolen it, and placed it on his head,
feeming to be much pleafed with his dexterity; perhaps his opinion of ftealing was fimilar to that of the
Lacedæmonians.   None of thefe people exceeded five
feet ten inches in height, yet their bodies appeared
large and robuft, though their limbs were fmall.   They
had broad flat faces, low foreheads, high cheeks, nofes
inclining to flatnefs, wide noftrils, fmall black eyes,
large mouths, fmall but indifferent teeth, and black

ftrait

ftrait hair, falling down over their ears and foreheads,
which was commonly fmeared with brown and red
paints; and, like all the aboriginal natives of America,
they were beardlefs.   Their garments were the fkins
of guanicos and feals, which they wrapped round their
fhoulders, fometimes leaving the right arm bare.   The
men likewife wear on their heads a bunch of yarn,
fpun from the wool of guanicos, which falls over their
foreheads, and ties behind with the finews or tendons
of fome animal.   Many of both fexes were painted in
different parts of their bodies, with red, white, and
brown colours; and had alfo three or four perpendi-
cular lines pricked acrofs their cheeks and nofes.   The
women have a fmall ftring tied round each ancle, and
wear each a flap of fkin tied round the middle.
They carry the children on their backs, and are generally employed in domeftic labour and drudgery.

Thefe Indians have a village, confifting of thirteen
houfes, behind a hill on the South fide of the bay, and
about two miles from the fhore.   They are about fifty
in number, and feem to be the only inhabitants here,
as the adjacent country is entirely defolate: their huts
are but wretched habitations, and their food is chiefly
mufcles

mufcles and feals. Their arms are bows and arrows, which they employ with great dexterity; the bows are neatly made from a fpecies of wood refembling beech, and their arrows are formed of a light yellow wood, feathered at one end, and pointed at the other with fharp ftones of the jafper kind. They have dogs about two feet in height, with fharp ears, and appear not unacquainted with Europeans. From feveral rings and buttons in their poffeffion, we concluded them to have fome communication with the Indians in the Streights of Magellan.

The bay of Good Succefs extends Eaft and Weft three miles, being two in breadth: its foundings within are regular, from fourteen to four fathom, the ground being a dark brown fand, except within a cable's length of the fhore, where it is rocky and foul, with great quantities of fea-weed. It is well ftocked with wood and water, and defended from eafterly winds by Staten Land. At the bottom of the Weft part of the bay is a fine fandy beach. Befide Port Maurice, to the northward there is another bay with anchorage, between Cape St. Vincent and St. Diego.

Le

Le Maire's ftreight towards the North end is formed by Cape St. Antonio on Staten Land, and Cape St. Vincent on Terra del Feugo; and towards the South by Cape St. Bartholemew on Staten Land, and a high bluff or prominence of Terra del Feugo, paffing between them; it is about nine leagues in length, and fix or feven in breadth. The tide flows therein feven hours from the northward, and ebbs five hours from the fouthward; and the ftream appears to divide itfelf, one part running along Terra del Feugo, and the other along Staten Land. The mountains on both fides of this ftreight are not fo very high as has been reprefented; neither are they always covered with fnow, except in particular places.

Having furnifhed ourfelves with twenty tons of wood and water, and ftowed our guns and other kinds of lumber below decks, that we might be prepared for the tempeftuous weather which might be expected in paffing Cape Horn, we left the bay of Good Succefs on the 21ft of January, at two o'clock P. M. and ftood to fea; the wind being at S. W. by W. we fteered at S. S. E. and the 22d, the wind becoming at W. we failed S. Monday the 23d, at four P. M. we difcovered the land, at W. S. W. appearing in three iflands. The 24th the

land

land appeared making in feveral fmall iflands at Weft; we founded in forty fathoms; the air was at the fame time extremely cold. The 25th we faw Le Maire's Cape Horn at S. W. by S. five leagues diftant: it appears to be a low point, and is the S. E. extremity of feveral iflands, called by the French Ifles d'Hermitage; near it are feveral pointed ragged rocks. This cape is in latitude $55^\circ 48'$ S. and longitude $67^\circ 40$ W. the variation $21^\circ 16'$ E. the dipping-needle ftood at $64^\circ 30'$. We founded in fifty-five fathoms, round ftones and broken fhells at bottom. We difcovered a point of land northward from Cape-Horn, which we concluded to be the ifland mentioned by Le Maire, and called Barnevelts or Diego Ramiries. We had about this time but little night; a favourable circumftance in the fqually difagreeable weather which then prevailed.

On the 30th of January we found ourfelves in latitude $60^\circ 2$ S. and longitude $73^\circ 5$ W. variation $24^\circ 54$. E. This was our higheft fouthern latitude; and from thence we changed our courfe to W. N. W. without much variation, having pleafant weather until the 16th of February, when the wind blew hard from W. by S. S. b. W. and S. Continuing our courfe N. W. between the 4th and 10th of March at nights we had very

F   heavy

heavy dews, almoft equal to fhowers of rain. On the 21ft we obferved great numbers of tropic and egg-birds; two of the former were killed, and found their feathers of a very beautiful colour, confifting of a moft delicate white tinged with a lively red. The tail is compofed of two long red feathers, and the beak is of a deep red colour. At this time we were in latitude 25° 21 S and longitude 120° 20 W. the weather being very pleafant, and the air ferene, dry, and falubrious. Continuing our courfe north-wefterly, between the Dolphin's firft and fecond track, on Tuefday the 4th of April we difcovered land at South, diftant four leagues. At half paft twelve we brought too, and founded, but found no ground at one hundred and thirty fathoms. The land then appeared to be an ifland, divided into four parts by reefs, and bore S. S. W. two miles diftant. The inhabitants at the firft divifion appeared naked, and about thirty in number; fome of them however appeared cloathed a little after. On fhewing our colours feveral of them came into the water, and by figns defired us to come on fhore; and as we paffed towards the fecond divifion they followed us along the water fide. Their complexion was a deep copper colour, and their hair black and ftrait; they were all armed with lances. This ifland is about two

6

miles

miles and a half in length, and in latitude 18° 44, and longitude 138° 58 Weft; we named it Lagone; and obferved it to be covered with cocoa-nut, palm, and plantain-trees, fome of which appeared vary high. At half paft three the fame afternoon we difcovered another ifland, lying N. W. twenty miles diftant from Lagone, and failed within a furlong of the fhore; the ifland appearing to be oval in its form, and about one mile in length; it was well covered with trees, but we faw no appearance of inhabitants: even approaching we loft fight of it. The next morning at fix we faw a low ifland at Eaft, about three leagues in length; the Eaft end was covered with very high trees, under which we obferved feveral huts, canoes, and Indians. At the Weft end there is a reef, extending three or four miles from the land; we called this Bird Ifland; it is in latitude 17° 24 S. and longitude 142° 50 W. The 8th we faw an ifland, which we named Chain-Ifland, in latitude 17° 24 and longitude 145° 26'.

Monday the 10th of April, in the morning we faw Oznabrug Ifland, bearing N. W. by W. half W. fix leagues diftant; and leaving it to the northward, at noon we difcovered George's Ifland from the maintop-maft head, and ftood towards it; but having little

wind

wind, it was the 13th in the morning when we came to anchor in Port Royal bay; and immediately after the captain went on fhore in the long-boat, attended by the marines, but returned again in the afternoon, having feen no perfon of any diftinction or confideration among the natives, though he had prefented a few beads and other trifles to fome of them. The next morning feveral of the officers and gentlemen landed on the weftermoft part of the bay, where they were treated with great hofpitality by the natives, who gave them provifions dreft in their own manner, with fome pieces of cloth manufactured by themfelves, and afterwards conducted them through feveral parts of the ifland.

It happened in this tour that Dr. Solander loft an opera-glafs, which had been greatly admired by feveral of the natives, and which he therefore fufpected to have been ftolen by fome of them; and this fufpicion he communicated by figns to a chief of one of the diftricts, informing him at the fame time that the place where he had miffed it was at fome diftance. The chief appeared much concerned at this accident; not, as we had reafon afterwards to believe, that he had any averfion from knavifh practices, but becaufe he

feared

feared that this early inftance of difhonefty might give us unfavourable fufpicions of his countrymen, and thereby deprive them of thofe advantages and emoluments which they expected to gain from us, and which by various artifices they afterwards fecured, when our connexion with them became more intimate. The chief. therefore, to obviate any difadvantageous impreffions, gave us to underftand, with an appearance of great probity, that the place which the Doctor had mentioned was not within his diftrict, but that he would fend to the chief of it, and endeavour if poffible to have the glafs recovered; but that if this could not be done, he would make the Doctor compenfation by giving him as much new cloth, of which he fhewed large quantities, as fhould be thought equal to its value. The cafe however was in a little time brought, and the glafs itfelf foon after, which deprived us of the merit we fhould otherwife have had in refufing the cloth which had been offered us. But it afforded an opportunity of convincing the natives of our generofity, by lavifhing rewards on them for an action to which felf-intereft had been the motive, rather than any fentiment of probity; to which, from numerous tranfactions, I am convinced they are ftrangers. And indeed we behaved with fuch liberality, or rather prodigality towards them in the

firft

part of our ftay here, that they were encouraged to
form the moft exorbitant claims and expectations from
us, and to contrive numerous artifices to defraud us;
which, with a little early œconomy and circumfpection
might have been prevented, greatly to our advantage.
Very different however was our opinion of thefe people
at the return of our boat in the evening, when every
one was agreeably furprifed at the great probity which
they feemed to have difcovered; though we were not
a little difappointed in the expectations we had formed
of procuring a large fupply of hogs and fowls, which,
from the report made by the Dolphin's crew, we had a
right to expect; but we found eventually that this report
like many others from the fame quarter, was extravagant; as all the fupplies obtained here afforded us no
more than the inconfiderable allowance of one pound
of frefh pork per week to each man.

The third day after our arrival feveral chiefs of the
ifland came on board, and brought with them a few
hogs, and a fmall quantity of fruit. The following
day we marked out a place for erecting a fortification
to fecure us in obferving the tranfit of Venus, for
which we were to wait; and at the fame time pitched
our tents, &c. on fhore, planting centinels to guard

                                                    our

our tools and utenfils, who were directed to fuffer none
of the natives to come within certain limits; one of the
marines however being carelefs, and willing to amufe
himfelf with their droll geftures and attitudes, allowed
feveral of them to approach him too nearly, who fuddenly wrefted the mufket out of his hands, and endeavoured to ftab him with the bayonet, and afterwards efcaped to the woods. One of them, however,
who was the firft aggreffor, was fhot through the head
in creeping among the bufhes, by a party fent in purfuit of them; two or three others were likewife wounded, as we were afterwards informed, though no intel-
ligence could ever be procured of the mufket which
they had carried off.

Immediately after this tranfaction we ftruck our
tents, and the fame evening conveyed every thing on
board; and the next morning we unmoored, and warped our fhip to a place more convenient for covering our
intended fortification; and again moored at the diftance
of half a mile from the fhore, with two thirds of a
cable extended each way; and then carried a ftream-
anchor towards the fhore for a fpring, bringing the
cable to our larboard quarter, and thereby made our
broadfide bear on the place we intended to fortify.

The

The next day we again fent out tents on fhore, together with all our empty water-cafks, which were filled,
and placed fo as to form a breaft-work on that part of
the beach which was flanked by a river; and on the
other we erected banks of earth, and covered them
with pallifades, mounting feveral cannon and fwivels
which had been landed from the fhip, for our protec-
tion.　Being thus fecured, we eftablifhed a market,
where the natives frequently brought fruit and provifions, which they bartered with us for iron utenfils,
beads, &c. though this traffic was by an order from
the captain foon reftrained to a fingle perfon appointed
by himfelf.　Having at this time but little employ-
ment, we frequently made incurfions into the country,
vifiting the natives at their habitations, where we were
always received with great hofpitality; though it happened not unfrequently that our pockets were picked by
thofe who had voluntarily given us large fupplies of
provifions.　This ifland, which the commander of the
Dolphin twenty-gun-fhip had named King George's
Ifland, is by the natives called Otahitee; and confifts
of two peninfulas, joined by an ifthmus.　The greater
peninfula is called Otahitee-Nua, and the leffer Otahi-
tee-Eta.　The former indeed is fometimes called Obrea-
bo, in honour to queen Obrea.　The whole length of
the

the ifland is fifteen leagues, and its circumference forty
leagues ; Port Royal bay is fituated near the Weft end.
From thence the coaft extends Eaft by South, about nineteen miles, to a reef of three fmall iflands, forming a bay
called Society Bay. From this the land inclines into a deep
bay at the ifthmus or juncture of the two divifions, of
which the fmalleft is nearly oval, and furrounded by a
reef, which runs parallel to the fhore, at about two miles
diftance ; this has feveral apertures or paffages which afford fafe anchorage within. The North fide of the ifland
is likewife defended by a fimilar reef, but the ground
within is foul and unfafe for veffels of burthen.

The foil of the ifland, on the more elevated parts, is
dry, and confifts of a red loam, which is very deep;
but the vallies are covered with a fertile black mould.
The ifland is under the government of a fingle chief,
whofe authority is unlimited, and who appoints depu-
ties that prefide in different diftricts, to preferve good
order, and collect thofe impofitions or duties, which
by long eftablifhment have become his due. And
though no particular laws have been enacted among
them, yet certain penalties or punifhments, from long
ufage and ancient cuftom, are annexed to certain crimes
or mifdemeanors. Thus, for example, thofe who

G

fteal

steal clothes or arms, are commonly put to death, either by hanging or drowning in the sea; but those who steal provisions are bastinadoed. By this practice they wisely vary the punishment of the same crime, when committed from different motives; judging, perhaps, that he who steals cloth or arms, steals because he is either idle or avaricious, qualities which probably will always continue with the offender to the disturbance of society; but he who steals from hunger is impelled by one of the most important desires of nature, and will not offend again, unless the same impulse recurs, which it is not likely will often happen.

The natives of Otahitee are unequal in stature, some of them being six feet and three inches in height, others not more than five feet and a half; commonly however they are tall and large in size, but not strong and vigorous; their joints being more flexible than those of the most delicate European women I have ever seen. From infancy they habituate themselves to dancing, according to their own peculiar mode, which consists of very extravagant distortions and gesticulations, together with various inflexions of their bodies and limbs, which being frequently practised, seem, like the effect of early habit in our tumblers, to be the cause of that enlarged

motion

motion in their joints, which prevents their attaining a
degree of ftrength proportionate to their fize.   In fit-
ting they commonly incline very much forward, but
in walking they carry themfelves very erect, even
when advanced in old age.

Their complection is brown, but much lighter than
that of the natives of America; fome few among them
appeared almoft as white as Europeans, and feveral had
red hair, though it is commonly black and ftrait.

Their garments are made from cloth manufactured
by themfelves from a vegetable fubftance produced by
a tree, which we named the cloth-tree.   Thefe garments vary in their figure, and in the manner in which
they are worn; circumftances, which though regulated
with fuch rigid exactnefs in European countries, with
them depend on fancy, caprice, or the ftate of the weather, as to heat, cold, rain, &c.   In the day time they
have always a covering about the pubes; and in dry pleafant weather they commonly wear a piece of thin cloth,
about two yards in length, having a perforation or hole
in the middle, through which the head is paffed, and
which hangs loofely over the fhoulders; but when in
their houfes this cloth is frequently taken from the

G 2   neck,

neck, and rolled about their loins. The women esteem it as most ornamental to enfold the pubes with many windings of cloth, which they draw so close about the middle, and round the upper part of their thighs, that it is a confiderable impediment to them in walking. Both sexes indent or prick the flesh about and below the hips in a multitude of places, with the points of sharp bones, and these indentures they fill with a dark blue or blackish paint, which ever after continues, and discolours the skin in those places, rendering it black. This practice is universal among them, and is called tat-tow, a term which they afterwards applied to letters when they saw us write, being themselves perfectly illiterate. The men have long hair, which they tie on the top of their heads, sticking it with plumage of birds; but the hair of the women is short, and hangs in curls down the neck; and both sexes frequently wear pieces of white cloth of their own manufacture wrapped about their heads, almost in the form of a turban. The females with infinite labour plait human hair into long small chords or threads, which they fold into bunches, and tie as an ornament over their foreheads; so powerful and universal are the emotions of vanity! They likewise wear ear-rings of

pearl,

pearl, as well as the men, but no bracelets or neck-laces.

The men, unlike the aborigines of America, have long beards, which they carefully drefs in different forms. And, notwithftanding Mofes has reprefented circumci-fion as injoined by the Deity to Abraham, for a diftin-guifhing mark or criterion appropriated to him and his pofterity the Jews, yet the natives of this ifland uni-verfally practice it from notions of cleanlinefs, having a term of reproach which they apply to the uncircum-cifed, but which decency will not allow me to repeat.

Though they have made but little progrefs towards civilization and refinement, yet they are already di-vided into the conditions of mafters and fervants; fo naturally do the paffions of mankind lead them to af-pire to dominion; and fo eafily do the differences in their bodily and intellectual faculties enable fome of them to obtain it to the detriment of the reft, who are made fubfervient to them. Almoft all the freemen of Otahitee have feveral of thefe fervants about their houfes, who are the moft dexterous thieves and pick-pockets perhaps in the whole world, as we often found to our difadvantage; but yet it muft be acknowledged

that

that they were not wantonly difhoneft, but as often as they ftole things that were ufelefs to themfelves, which frequently happened, they either voluntarily brought them back to their owners, or laid them in places where they muft be neceffarily found; thus, for in-ftance having in the night, with great fecrecy and dexterity, found means to enter our encampment unper-ceived, and carry away our aftronomical quadrant, which was indefpenfably neceffary for thofe obferva-tions that were a principal object of the voyage; after keeping and examining it a few days, and finding it to be ufelefs to themfelves, one from among them was commiffioned to intimate to us that he had feen one of his countrymen carry and hide it under a certain tree, which he defcribed, but declared he did not know the thief; however on examining the place he had mentioned, we found the quadrant, a little difordered by handling and infpection, though the damage was foon repaired.

The women of Otahitee have agreeable features, are well proportioned, fprightly, and lafcivious; neither do they efteem continence as a virtue, fince almoft every one of our crew procured temporary wives among them, who were eafily retained during our ftay. The inhabitants

inter-

intermarry with each other for life, but with this fingular circumftance, that as foon as a man has taken a wife he is excluded the fociety of the women, and of the unmarried of his own fex, at the time of their meals, being compelled to eat with his fervants. For this reafon they are not folicitous to attach themfelves to a fingle object, during the earlier part of life, but purfue incontinent gratifications where inclination leads, until a woman becomes pregnant, when the father by long eftablifhed cuftom is compelled to marry her.

The chief or fovereign of the ifland is allowed but one wife, though he has many concubines: the favage policy of government however requires that all his natural children be put to immediate death as foon as born, to preclude the diforders which might arife from a competition for the fucceffion. The badge of fovereignty is called Maro, which is a kind of red fafh worn about the middle. When the Erei or chief is firft invefted with this mark of his authority, the ceremony is attended with an extraordinary feftival, which continues the fpace of three days. The Erei when he has been invefted with the Maro is ever after fed by his attendants, who take his food in their fingers, and put it in his
mouth,

mouth, dipping them in a bowl of cocoa nut milk before each mouthful.

The inhabitants of Otahitee may be computed at feventy thoufand. They believe the exiftence of one fupreme God, whom they call Maw-we, but acknowledge an infinite number of inferior deities generated from him, and who prefide over particular parts of the creation. *Maw we* is the being who fhakes the earth, or the god of earthquakes. They have however no religious eftablifhment, or mode of divine worfhip; neither the dictates of nature or of reafon having fuggefted to them the expediency or propriety of paying external adoration to the deity: on the contrary, they think him too far elevated above his creatures, to be affected by their actions. They have indeed certain funeral rites, and other ceremonies, for which a certain order of men are appropriated, though they have no immediate relation to the deity, and thefe men we called priefts, but perhaps not with much propriety. They have fome notion of a future life in another ifland, to which they expect to be tranflated after death; but it does not feem as if they confidered it as a ftate of retribution for the actions of this life, fince they believe that each individual will there enjoy the

fame

fame condition in which he has lived here, whether it be that of a prince, a mafter, or a fervant. They believe the ftars to be generated between the fun and moon, and fuppofe an eclipfe to be the time of copulation. They likewife fuppofe the greateft part of the earth or main land to be placed at a great diftance eaftward, and that their ifland was broken or feparated from it while the deity was drawing it about the fea, before he refolved upon its fituation.

Though thefe people have no particular mode of divine worfhip, we frequently obferved that in eating they cut a fmall piece of their food and depofited in fome retired place as an offering to Maw-we.

When any difputes arife among the people concerning property, the ftrongeft retains poffeffion, but the weaker complains to the Erei, who, from a political defire of maintaining equality among his fubjects, generally gives it to the pooreft of the contending parties.

Their funeral rites are of a fingular kind; the dead body is depofited in a houfe built for that purpofe at fome diftance from the common habitation of the fa-

H   mily,

mily, and laid on a floor elevated feveral feet above the ground, being covered with fine cloth; then a kind of prieft, called Heavah, cloathed in a mantle covered with gloffy feathers, and commonly attended with two boys painted black, ftrews the body with flowers and leaves of bambo, and carries prefents of fifh, and other food, which he depofits by the fide of it, and for two or three days after is conftantly employed in ranging the adjacent woods and fields, from which every one retires on his approach. The relations in the mean time build a temporary houfe, contiguous to that which contains the corpfe, where they affemble, and the females mourn for the deceafed by finging fongs of grief, howling, and wounding their bodies in diffe-rent places, after which they bathe their wounds in the fea or river, and again return to howl and cut themfelves, which they continue for three days. After the body is corrupted, and the bones become naked or bare, the fkeleton is depofited in a kind of ftone pyra-mid built for that purpofe *.

* In a retired part of the ifland we obferved one of thefe pyramids, of a much larger fize than the reft, which was compofed of huge rough ftones laid on each other, and which probably contained the bones of fome ancient prince or hero; on the top were the beaks of feveral large birds, and the bones of fifh, which had probably been offered as prefents to the deceafed.

A con-

A confiderable part of Otahitee is cultivated and planted with cocoa-nut trees, plantains, and bananoes, cloth-trees, bread-trees, yams, and potatoes like thofe of Europe, which have however a bitterifh tafte. Their animal food confifts of fifh of various kinds, which they take in different ways, and with great dexterity; thefe they frequently eat raw, a practice in which fome of our people imitated them, and thought it not unpalatable; they likewife feed on fwine, of which they have a confiderable plenty, but prefer the flefh of dogs to that of all other animals. They have alfo wild ducks, which differ but very little from thofe of Europe. They roaft or rather bake their meat in a fubterraneous oven, made by digging a hole in the ground and lining it with a ftone bottom; in this they kindle a fire, and lay feveral loofe ftones upon it; when they are all fufficiently heated the fire and afhes are removed, and the meat being wrapped in leaves is placed in the oven, and the hot loofe ftones laid immediately upon it, and the whole is then covered over with earth; in this manner it is excellently dreffed, retaining all its fucculency: they have no falt, but inftead of it ufe fea-water. They are immoderate eaters, and fwallow large mouthfuls at once. Inftead of bread they eat yams, potatoes, plantains, &c. together with

a large

a large milky farinaceous fruit, which when baked refembles bread both in texture and tafte. They make a kind of pafte from the pulp or white fubftance adhering to the infide of the cocoa-nut fhell and bananas, which commonly ferves them for fupper and breakfaft: their common drink is water and the milk or juice of cocoa-nuts. They have no kind of fpiritous liquor, except that which is made from a fpecies of pepper growing here, which they ferment in water; but this is fo fcarce that it is rarely drank, except by the chiefs of the country. They have none among them who pretend to any kind of medical knowledge which is not common to every body. They have indeed but few difeafes, and to thefe they apply but a few empirical remedies, which from experience they think ufeful, without knowing or enquiring concerning the manner of their operation. Their inftruments of mufic are a large drum, and a kind of flute, made from the joint of a reed, having three perforations or holes, which is blown through the nofe. Their fifh-hooks are of various fizes; thofe for taking fharks are very large, and made from heavy folid wood, of a proper figure, and pointed. They have fmaller hooks, made likewife from wood, and pointed with bones, which are commonly barbed: befides thefe they have a variety

of

of very fmall hooks, made of different circular figures, from mother of pearl. Their lines are made from the fibres of the bark of a tree, which compofes almoft all their cordage.

The cloth of Otahitee, of which large quantities are manufactured, is of a fingular kind, being made from the bark of a fmall tree, which is firft freed from its external hard coat, and then, being fcraped or rafped, it is foaked or macerated in water two or three days, when after a little beating it becomes glutinous and cohefive like pafte, but more tenacious; and is then extended or fpread by beating it with an inftrument made for that purpofe from a very compact heavy wood. This inftrument is about fifteen inches in length, and from the handle at one end to the other of equal fize, and about fix inches in circumference; its form is quadrangular, and each of the four fides is furrowed into longitudinal grooves or finuffes, but with this difference, that there is a regular gradation in the breadth and depth of the furrows on each of the fides; the coarfeft angle contains about ten of thefe furrows, and the fineft about fixty: the bark is extended by beating with this inftrument in the fame manner as gold is formed into leaves by the hammer. They begin beat-

2

ing

ing with that fide where the channels are deepeft and wideft, and proceeding regularly they finifh with that where they are moft numerous, which leaves the appearance of longitudinal furrows or channels on the cloth much like thofe which are vifible on paper, but a little deeper. This cloth is commonly beat until it becomes very thin; when they defire it thicker two or three pieces are fpread on each other and pafted together: by bleaching they render it extremely white, and often ftain it red, yellow, brown, and black. That which is worn by thofe who are mourning for the death of a relation is double, the infide being white, and the other brown, with black fpots laid on pretty clofely in chequers. This cloth, though made in fo fimple a manner, has notwithftanding a confiderable degree of ftrength and firmnefs, and might doubtlefs be highly ufeful in the manufacture of paper. They fold it to us for trifling confiderations; as feveral yards might be purchafed for a fingle nail. Their breaft-plates are of a femicircular figure, and have each a notch of a femicircular form in the middle of the fection. The breaft-plate confifts of an internal wicker frame, which is covered with a ftrong cloth or clofe plexus, made from the fibres contained in the rinds of cocoa-nuts braided together; over this are laid three

femi-

femicircular rows of pigeon's feathers, and between each is a femicircular row of fhark's teeth. The edge of the breaft-plate is fringed with fine white hair, and feveral parts of it are ornamented with round pieces of mother of pearl, about two inches in diameter. One of thefe plates hangs from the neck down before the breaft, and a fecond depends over the back.

Their hatchets are made by tying a fharp hard ftone, appearing like a jafper, but more like the touch-ftone, to the end of a wooden handle, which when finifhed is near the fhape of a fmall garden hoe.

Their bows are round, and tapering from the middle towards each end; they are about five feet and a half in length, and made from a light but ftrong elaftic wood. Their arrows are a fmall compact ftrong fpecies of reed or bamboo, and pointed fometimes with hard folid wood, and fometimes with a fharp bearded bone, taken from the fting-ray fifh. They have likewife a kind of fpears or javelins, made from wood, but pointed after the manner of their arrows, which they throw with great dexterity.

The

The natives of Otahitee vifit the iflands lying to the eaftward, which we had difcovered in our paffage hither, for the fake of traffic, in their canoes, waiting the opportunity of winds, which blow favourably about three months every year. With the inhabitants of thofe iflands they barter their cloth and provifions for pearl and a fine white hair, which grows on a fpecies of dogs peculiar to themfelves, and with this they ornament their breaft-plates.

Soon after our arrival at Otahitee we found that this ifland had been fome months before vifited by a foreign fhip under Spanifh colours, as the natives informed us, after we had fhewn them all the feveral European flags. And at Batavia we difcovered that this vifitor was no other than Monfieur Bougainville, who lately returned from a voyage round the world, which he undertook by the direction and at the expence of the court of France. From the accounts of the natives it appears that the French conducted themfelves peaceably, until fome of the inhabitants had ftolen the cloaths belonging to three of the fhip's crew, who were bathing, and on its being difcovered had murdered them; upon which their companions falling on the Indians, had killed one,

one and taken another prifoner, who was carried away
from the ifland.

It was not long after our people began to cohabit
with the females of Otahitee, before they difcovered,
by difagreeable effects, that the crew of the French fhip
had before enjoyed the favours of feveral of their temporary wives, who in return infected them with a certain difeafe.

On the 4th of June, the fky being unufually ferene, our aftronomer had a very accurate obfervation
of the tranfit of Venus; and foon after we began to
prepare for leaving the ifland to proceed on our voyage; and about the fame time two officers belonging
to the fhip, having been long engaged in a quarrel,
which had created much difturbance on board, agreed
to terminate the difpute by a duel; and having furnifhed themfelves with arms and ammunition, they
landed privately, but after a few difcharges they were
arrefted and reconducted on board, by a party fent for
that purpofe, before any mifchief had happened.

During our ftay, Mr. Banks and Dr. Solander, who
were indefatigable in their refearches after natural know-

I   ledge,

ledge, had collected a great variety of undescribed plants and fish, with some birds, &c. and we had made a considerable progress in learning the language of the country, which, like that of almost all nations living between the tropics, is soft, usually terminating in vowels. We had likewise planted many European seeds, of which none, except mustard, cresses, and melons, were found to vegetate: and having furnished ourselves with sufficient specimens of the cloth, implements, and utensils of Otahitee, together with sufficient supplies of wood and water, on the 13th of July, 1769, we sailed from George's Island, having on board an Indian named Tobia, who had formerly been high-priest of Otahitee, but being disgusted with the present regent, he voluntarily embarked on our voyage, bringing with him an Indian lad named Tiato, as an attendant. On leaving Otahitee we sailed to a small island, which we had seen from the hills of George's Island, and which is called by the natives Titeroah. It is a group of seven small keys, and belongs to the sovereign of Otahitee, from which he procures fish, turtle, &c. being situated seven leagues North from Port Royal bay, in latitude 17° 10′ S. and longitude 150° 00 W.

From

From Titeroah we failed north-weft, and the next
day faw the high lands of an ifland, which Tobia informed us was called by the natives Ulyateah; but this
and the following day we had very little wind.   The
17th we fteered towards an ifland, called by the natives
Oahena, and a few hours after anchored in a very pleafant bay called Owarre, where we continued two days.
The ifland of Oahena is fourteen leagues in circuit,
nor can the moft exuberant fancy conceive a more de-
lightful fpot: the fhores were adorned with fruit-trees
of various kinds, efpecially the cocoa-nuts, which we
faw in abundance.   The foil is extremely fertile, the
trees fruitful, and affording the moft beautiful land-
fcapes: it is one of the dependencies of Opuna a neighbouring fovereign.   The inhabitants are well proportioned, with regular engaging features; the women
in particular are uncommonly delicate and beautiful.
They behaved towards us with great probity and hofpitality, felling us for trifling confiderations large fupplies of hogs, poultry, fifh, fruit, &c.   They were
much furprifed at the fight of our fhip, it being the
firft they had ever feen; and it was not without great
difficulty that we perfuaded them to venture into the
cabin, where they viewed every thing with an appearance
of pleafure and aftonifhment.

From

From Oahena we failed westerly; and the next day, being the 20th, anchored in a bay, called by the inhabitants Oapoah, situated on the North side of an island to which Tobia had directed us, and which he named Uliateah, being in latitude 16° 47′ S. and longitude 151° 40′ W. North-westerly from this is another island, called by the natives Otahaw, being ten leagues distant, and in latitude 16° 37′ S. and longitude 151° 45′ W. Both of these islands are surrounded by a reef or shoal, which defends their bays or harbours, and affords fafe anchorage. The entrance into the bay of Oapoah is near a small island towards the West end: within the bay are several shoals of coral rock, but as they are visible they may be easily avoided.

On the 24th weighing anchor, we steered northward along shore, and within the shoal, towards an opening, five or six leagues distant, through which we passed, and being without the reef, began to beat round the island of Otahaw, which employed us eight days; in which time we sent our boat to the south-west part of the island, where there is passage through the surrounding shoal, and a good harbour within. Otahaw is about twelve leagues in circuit, and the land is high, rugged,

rugged, and woody, furrounded with fmall iflands or keys on the Weft fide.

On the 2d of Auguft we anchored in a bay on the North fide of Uliateah, which is called by the natives O a-ma-ne-no, where we continued eight days, having moored our fhip about two cables length from the fhore.

Uliateah is a fruitful ifland, near forty leagues in circuit, and well watered with rivers; the natives appeared hofpitable and honeft, felling us a good ftore of hogs, wild ducks, bread, fruit, &c. On the Weft fide of Uliateah, at nine or ten leagues diftance, we difcovered an ifland called Mo-ro-ah, which is near the fize of Otahaw, but has no harbour.

In beating round Otahaw we difcovered an ifland a few leagues to the weftward, named, as Tobia informed us, Bola Bola, which is about ten leagues in circumference, and remarkable for a high double peak ; but it has no harbour on the Weft fide. This ifland, according to Tobia's information, is rocky and barren, and was not inhabited until the fovereigns of Otahitee and the neighbouring iflands banifhed their criminals
thither,

thither, which was practiſed for ſeveral years; and they
being increaſed by others, who voluntarily fled thither
to avoid puniſhment, became ſo numerous that the
iſland was inſufficient for their ſubſiſtence; and they
thereupon became pirates, ſeizing every canoe that fell
in their power.   Their government was at firſt feudal,
until Opuna their preſent ſovereign had the addreſs to
deprive his fellow-ſoldiers of their freedom; and to
prevent them from reflecting on his uſurpation, as well
as to revenge the contempt with which he was treated
by the neighbouring inhabitants, he made a deſcent
upon Otahaw, which he ſoon conquered; and, encouraged by this ſucceſs, he landed on Uliateah, where
the inhabitants bravely exerted themſelves in defence
of their liberty and of their chief, who was greatly
beloved.   The war however continued three years, with
various ſucceſs, until at length Opuna becoming more
ſucceſsful, the ſovereign of Uliateah was killed, leaving
an infant ſon, who was immediately inveſted with the
Maro on the only eminence which remained in the poſſeſſion of his ſubjects.   But a deciſive victory ſoon after
putting Opuna in poſſeſſion of the whole iſland, the
young king fled to Otahitee, where he was hoſpitably
received and reſpectfully treated, having a part of the
iſland allotted to him and his followers, in which he

lived

lived according to the manner of James II. while at
St. Germains

Opuna afterwards conquered feveral other neighbouring iflands, which he annexed as dependencies to his
dominion of Bolla-Bolla; and which he ftill retains in
fubjection, being near ninety years of age.

It was of Uliateah that Tobia was a native, and fub-
ordinate chief; and being wounded in the laft decifive
battle with Opuna, he fled to the mountains until his
wounds were cured, and then followed the young king
to Otahitee, where he ingratiated himfelf even to the
laft favours with Obrea, the then queen regent of the
ifland, who appointed him high prieft, and purfued
his advice in almoft every particular. But foon after
Tutahaw, uncle to the young king her fon, and a man
of great courage, and highly efteemed by the people,
obferving her devoted to amorous dalliance with Tobia,
meditated a change in the regency; and the better to
effect it, he began to create divifions between the inhabitants of Otahite-Eta and of Otahite-Nua, which finally
produced hoftilities between them. At that time Tobia,
who had great fagacity and judgment, having difcovered Tutahaw's defigns, advifed the queen to procure his

death

death privately, as the only expedient to reftore peace and preferve her authority; but fhe thinking his advice too cruel, refufed, for the firft time, to comply with it; and he forefeeing the confequences, retired to the mountains, alledging that this retreat was neceffary for the prefervation of his life. Soon after the inhabitants of Leffer Otahitee making frequent incurfions into the greater divifion, and their numerous depredations having thrown the inhabitants of the latter into confufion, which Tutahaw artfully improving to his advantage, they at length offered him the regency, thinking their affairs too much embarraffed for the adminiftration of a female; an agreement was therefore made between Obrea and Tutahaw, in which it was conditioned, that fhe fhould preferve the title and ftate of queen, with a certain number of attendants, &c. and that the regency fhould devolve to Tutahaw; who refpecting Tobia's underftanding and facerdotal character, afterwards permitted him to return from the mountains in fafety; but he was fo much difpleafed with this revolution, that he embraced the opportunity of our departure to leave the ifland.

It deferves to be remembered, that when the Dolphin fhip of war firft difcovered George's Ifland, the

inha-

inhabitants, having never before feen a fhip, were un-determined how they fhould treat their new vifitors; and thereupon Obrea, who was then regent, called a council on the matter; and though it was finally re-folved to attack the fhip, and though this refolution was carried into execution; yet Obrea, whofe feelings were more congenial to the wants of mankind, pro-pofed, in direct oppofition to the advice of her coun-fellors, that a large fupply of women and hogs fhould be inftantly fent on board the fhip. A propofal fo pregnant with benevolent fenfibility, that it deferves to be recorded on tables of adamant; for what could have been more acceptable than women and hogs to failors, who had long been deprived of both?

We had intended vifiting Bola-Bola, but were pre-vented by an account which Tobia gave us of the fa-vage and inhofpitable difpofition of its inhabitants, who he affured us would attempt our deftruction. He likewife told us, that in the life-time of his grand-father a fhip had been wrecked on the ifland of Ulia-teah; and that the few of her crew who were not drown-ed were killed by the inhabitants; and that from this wreck they had procured the firft iron which had ever been feen among them, and formed it into chiffels, knives,

K &c.

&c. and indeed they appeared to have the higheſt value for this commodity, which we exchanged with
them for proviſion, fruit, &c.

Having completed our ſupply of wood, water, &c.
we ſailed from the bay of O-a-ma-ne-no on the 10th
of Auguſt, ſtanding ſouthwardly towards an iſland to
which Tobia directed us, at more than an hundred
leagues diſtance, and which we diſcovered on the 14th.
It is called O-hi-te-ro-ah by the natives, and is in latitude 22° 23′ S. and longitude 150° 36′ W. but having
no harbour, we only ſent our boat on ſhore without
coming to anchor.

Since our departure from Cape Horn we had diſcovered fourteen iſlands, all of them before unknown
in Europe; and Tobia had deſcribed nine others, lying
between W. N. W. and S. S. W. the fartheſt not more
than two days ſail, for a canoe, from Ohiteorah; beſides a very large one at Eaſt, diſtant about four days
ſail; all of which he had viſited in canoes at different
times. Ohiteroa is about eight leagues in circuit,
the greateſt part appearing to be covered with coarſe
graſs and fern; the bay is about a mile and a half in
breadth, and half a mile in depth, but foul and rocky.

From

From whence we failed South, fomewhat eaftwardly, and on Tuefday the 29th, at four o'clock in the morning, we faw a very large comet at north, about fixty degrees above the horizon; and the fame day at noon found ourfelves in latitude 36° 59¼'S. and longitude 4° 00'E. from Ohiteroah, variation 7° 9' Eaft. The following day we obferved a fmall green bird, which we judged to be an inhabitant of land, together with large quantities of fea-weed; and foon after feveral pentada birds, with many others of a fmaller fpecies, about the fize of a pigeon, having a white belly, brown back, and a black ftreak from the extremity of one wing to that of the other*. On Saturday the 2d of September, at half after four in the morning, we again obferved the comet between Aldebaran and Orion; and the fame day at noon found ourfelves in latitude 40° 14'S. and longitude 145° 26'W. The air being at that time very cold, and having hard gales, with many appearances of a long continuance of ftormy weather, we changed our courfe, and failed north-eafterly.

* It is not the writer's purpofe to defcribe minutely thofe things which are more particularly the objects of Natural Hiftory, as Mr. Banks and Dr. Solander, gentlemen of great erudition, who undertook this voyage for the fake of natural knowledge; and who in almoft every place were fuccefsful, as well as indefatigable, in their refearches, will hereafter abundantly gratify the curiofity of thofe who delight in the ftudy of nature.

Monday

Monday the 4th, at three o'clock in the morning, we faw the comet again, two degrees Eaft from the bright ftar in Orion's right foot; and at noon obferved in latitude 38° 29'S. and longitude 145° 14'W. The fame day we altered our courfe to N. N. W.

Wednefday the 6th at four o'clock in the morning we faw the comet, a little Eaft from Orion, for the laft time. We continued our courfe north-wefterly for feveral days, having good weather, and frequently feeing albatroffes, pentada birds, &c. in great numbers.

On the 20th of September, in latitude 29° 20'S. and longitude 150° 40'W. we again altered our courfe to South-Weft, having variable winds and weather. On the 25th we obferved a log of wood, feveral parcels of fea-weed, with albatroffes, pentadas, fheerwaters, &c. in great numbers.

Sunday the 1ft of October we took up a piece of timber covered with barnacles, and faw a feal fleeping on the water, feveral porpoifes, a grampus, numerous flocks of land-birds, and many parcels of rock-weed; we founded with one hundred and ninety fathom of line, but found no bottom. But continuing our courfe,

Saturday,

Saturday, October 7th, we difcovered land at Weft by North, which appeared in low hummocks; and at four o'clock P. M. the following day we anchored in a deep bay, with our beft bower, having ten fathom water, and a fine brown fandy bottom. This we called Poverty-Bay, it being on the Eaft fide of New Zealand, and in latitude 39° 00′ S. and longitude 179° 47′ Weft from Greenwich, and the variation 14° 30′ Eaft.

Wednefday the 11th, at feven P. M. the wind being wefterly, we left the bay, and failed to the fouthward, along the coaft, keeping at four or five miles diftance from the fhore. On Thurfday feveral of the natives came on board, and fold us fome of their paddles, cloth, &c. we made them feveral prefents, and they left us apparently well fatisfied with their reception. About twenty-two miles S. S. E. half E. from the North point or head of the bay is a cape, which, from its figure, we called Cape Table; between them we had regular foundings from thirteen to eighteen fathoms; but on ftanding four miles farther off from the cape we had feventy fathoms of water, with foft ground, being then on the outer edge of a bank that extends from the North head to Cape Table. About nine miles farther to the fouthward is a fmall ifland, which we named

Port-

Portland Ifle: it is connected to the main by a chain of
rocks, about a mile in length, which are partly under
water. About three miles N. E. from Portland are feveral fhoals, which we called the Shambles; one of thefe
we narrowly efcaped: there is however a paffage with
twenty fathom of water between them. On Friday
four large canoes came towards us filled with men, who
appeared to be all armed: they made feveral long
fpeeches, inviting or challenging us to battle; but
feeing themfelves difregarded, they boldly came along
fide, and threw their fpears into the fhip; we then
fired a mufket over them, which producing no effect,
we difcharged a four-pounder loaded with grape-fhot
above their heads, on which they precipitately retired.
But as we found the current fetting us faft towards
the fhore, we foon anchored in twenty-one fathom,
about a league diftant from the land.

On Saturday, the wind continuing at N. we failed
along the coaft, at about four miles diftance, having
from twelve to fifteen fathom of water. In the afternoon we fent our long-boat and pinnace afhore to
found, and difcover a watering-place, of which we had
great need; but they were foon recalled, as we faw
feveral canoes making towards them. Soon after
about

about one hundred and fifty of the armed natives in canoes approached us; and, to convince them of our pacific intentions, we threw feveral prefents into the water towards them, and employed every expedient in our power to allure them on board to trade; but all our endeavours were fruitlefs; and their defigns appeared more hoftile even than our former vifitors, as they actually proceeded to an attack upon us, and continued it, until, like the former, they were difperfed by the difcharge of a cannon, after which they fled to the fhore.   The next morning, being Sunday, we were near a very large bay, which we named Hawke's Bay, in latitude 39° 40′ S. and longitude 180° 30′ W. Here feveral fifhing-canoes came off with cray and other kinds of fifh, which we purchafed of them for paper and Otahitee cloth; but from their behaviour we concluded that they had never received any fentiment of probity, either from the fuggeftions of a moral fenfe, or the precepts of education; for after bargaining with us for a parcel of fifh, as often as they could get poffeffion of thofe commodities which they were to receive in payment, before they had tied their fifh to the rope by which we were to draw them on board, they would laugh at our want of precaution, and refolutely refufe us any return for what they had received, obliging us

to

to repurchafe the fame parcel of fifh with other paper
and cloth; and this without appearing to be fenfible
that there was any thing fhameful or unjuft in their
knavery; nor would any menace prevail with them
to alter their behaviour. While thefe fifhermen continued with us they were joined by feveral other canoes,
filled with armed natives; and as fome of our people
were trading for fifh over the fhip's fide, they made feveral attempts to force them into their canoes; and at
length they actually feized Tiato, the boy we had
brought from George's Ifland, and immediately fled
towards the fhore; we then fired feveral mufquets
among them, which obliged them to put on their
thick cloathing; and one of them feeing a gun pointed
at him, doubled up his nets, and held them before
him to intercept the ball. Several Indians however
being wounded in the canoe that had feized Tiato, he
found means to difengage himfelf and jump into the
water, but in fwimming towards the fhip he was purfued by a fecond canoe, that returned to retake him;
but to prevent this we difcharged a four-pounder a
little above their heads, on which they all retired; and
foon after the boy was taken up in a boat, which we
fent for that purpofe, but not before his ftrength was
almoft exhaufted, as his clothes, being thick and heavy,

                                                    had

had greatly impeded him in fwimming. He had doubtlefs but narrowly efcaped being eaten; though at that time we did not know that the inhabitants of New Zealand were cannibals. When this accident happened we were oppofite the South point of Hawke's Bay, which we from thence named Cape Kidnapper. There are two rocks lying without this cape, which are both of a conical form: Hawke's Bay enters within the land about thirteen leagues: near the middle, but towards the north fide, we obferved feveral fmall rivulets, and at the bottom a lagoon about three miles in breadth; its communication with the fea is by a fmall inlet at the north end, where the fea wafhes over, but apparently, there is not fufficient water for the entrance of any thing larger than canoes. The north fide is formed by a bank of fand extending to the fouthward; about the middle of this, is an elevation which has been converted to an ifland by the fands feparating or wearing away from it. It is about four miles in length, and one and an half in breadth, running from Eaft to Weft. The land near the bottom of the bay prefents a very beautiful profpect; being happily diverfified with large groves of tall ftrait trees, branching only towards the top, and refembling cedars: the more interior country rifes into mountains,

L   many

many of which are near as high as the Peak of Teneriffe, and covered on their tops with fnow. South-
weftward from thefe, the land appeared to be lefs elevated and uneven; as we difcovered feveral large level
plains, apparently covered with grafs.

From this bay we continued our courfe to the fouthward, until Tuefday noon, when we found ourfelves
in 40° 35′ South. It is to be remembered, that New
Zealand, before our arrival here, having been only
feen in two or three places, was but very imperfectly
known; and the Lords of the Admiralty being uncertain
whether it was an ifland or continent, had directed us
to fail along the coaft as far as 40° fouth latitude,
and from thence, if the land appeared to extend farther, to return again to the northward. And agreeable to thefe inftructions, at noon, being oppofite a
bluff or prominence of land, which we name Cape
Turnagain, we changed our courfe from South to
North; and the wind having likewife changed to the
fouthward, we returned nearly in our former track,
failing along the coaft about the fame diftance as ufual
from the fhore. Cape Turnagain is remarkable for a
ftratum of clay of a bright brown colour; its prominence gradually diminifhes towards the north-fide,

but

but to the fouthward its defcent is more fudden. The foundings oppofite to it, at the diftance of a mile and an half, are about thirty-two fathom, with coarfe yellow gravel at the bottom.

On Thurfday evening a canoe came along fide with five Indians who told us they intended to ftay all night : we therefore hoifted our guefts on board, and entertained them in the manner which we expected would be moft agreeable. There was nothing like ruftic bafhfulnefs or timidity in their behaviour; as they familiarly tafted of every thing which they faw us eat, even when uninvited; and appeared to have as much confidence in our hofpitality and friendfhip, as if they had long experienced both. Two of them were finely proportioned in their fhapes and limbs ; and their features appeared to have an unufual feminine delicacy. We difmiffed them the next morning with feveral prefents, and they left us with reluctance, being defirous to continue with us the whole day, to which we objected, thinking it fhould carry them too far from their habitations.

The next morning (having paffed the land which we firft difcovered on this coaft) we faw to the north-

ward

ward a bay with an ifland in the middle. In failing
into this bay between the ifland and the main, we had
very foul uneven ground, but afterwards the founding
became regular, and we anchored about half a mile
from the fhore in eight fathom, with a fine fandy bottom. Our boats were then fent in fearch of a watering place, but it being very fqually, with a great furf,
they could not land. In the afternoon we made a fecond attempt with more fuccefs; and the next morning
fent our boats for wood and water, with a party of men
to protect them. But the furf running high and finding great difficulty in bringing our water on board,
we gave over the attempt, and failed the next morning.
This bay is called Tegadoo Bay by the natives, who
did not appear to be numerous. It is in latitude 38°
11′ S. and longitude 180° 35′ W. The variation 13°
15′ E.

The inhabitants had a few houfes, furrounded by
a fence to intercept the winds, and feveral ftages for
drying fifh near the place at which we landed. They
appeared to have plenty of crabs, and cray-fifh, and a
great many dogs with fmall pointed ears. Some of
them were covered with cloth of their own manufacture,
which will be more particularly defcribed hereafter,

and

and several females had bunches of fea-weeds tied
about their middles. Continuing our courfe to the
northward, feveral canoes came along-fide, and fome
of them venturing on board, we enquired for a watering place, and they pointed to a bay, bearing S. W.
by W. to which we difpatched our boats, and at one
o'clock the fame afternoon they returned, having
found a convenient place for procuring a fupply
both of wood and water: and on Tuefday the 24th
we anchored in the bay, having ten fathom of water,
and a fandy bottom. The inhabitants here behaved
with great hofpitality. At the watering place we
drew a line, and enjoined them not to pafs it; an
injunction which they obeyed with great exactnefs.
There were feveral houfes contiguous, and the lands
in the adjacent vallies being regular flats, were neatly
difpofed in fmall plantations; the ground appearing
to be well broken as if defigned for gardens. Sweet
potatoes, like thofe of Carolina, of which they have
large quantities, commonly occupy a confiderable part
of thefe plantations. In many places we obferved the
cloth-plant growing without cultivation.

The bay itfelf affords plenty of fifh, particularly
cray-fifh, and fhip-jacks or horfe-makarel, which are
larger

larger than the makarel on the Britifh coaft.   The adjacent woods are very compact, and rendered almoft
impaffable by the numerous fupple jacks growing in
them.   But they afford fhelter to a multitude of birds
of different kinds, among which are the quail and a
very large pigeon.   We purchafed many things from
thefe people, efpecially cloth of their own manufacture,
giving them in exchange the cloth of Otahitee, of which
they were extravagantly fond.

Chaftity appeared not to be in great eftimation among
them; or, at leaft, it was not rigidly practifed, as
many of their young women conftantly reforted to the
watering place, who granted their laft favour to all-that
follicited them, and on very reafonable conditions.   In
rambling about the country we frequently met with
their habitations, and were always treated with great
kindnefs, as they never denied us any thing in their
poffeffion.   In one of thefe excurfions an officer fell in
with a group of houfes, and an elderly woman came
out and invited him to enter the enclofure, where he
found about two dozen of the natives, of both fexes,
feated at a repaft of cray-fifh and potatoes, of which he
was invited to partake; and having made them a fmall
prefent of cloth and beads, they fingled out a beautiful
                                                                young

young girl, and gave him to underſtand that he
might retire with her. Some time after, an elderly
man, with two women, entered, as viſitors, with much
gravity, and very formally ſaluted all the company
according to the cuſtom of the country; that is, by
gently joining the tips of their noſes, which a ſpectator
might miſtake for a kiſs: At parting, however, he re-
peated this ceremony, which gave them great plea-
ſure: and in returning the way by which he had come,
they ſent a man who lead him a much better road; the
other being in many places overflowed with water; and
in conducting him to the watering place, as often as they
came to a ditch or a rivulet, of which there are many
for draining their fields, the Indian always carried him
over dry, and appeared deſirous of tranſporting him the
whole way on his back. This bay is called Tolaga by
the natives, and is in latitude 38° 20′, and longitude
181° 38′ W. the variation being 13° 20′ E.

After completing our proviſion of wood and water,
and making an inſcription on a tree a little to the right
of our watering place, it being Sunday the 29th of October, at ſix in the morning, we ſailed from Tolaga
Bay, coaſting to the Northward: On the 31ſt ſeveral
canoes came towards us, one of them carrying ſixty of

the

the natives; but finding them determined on commit-
ting hoftilities, we difperfed them by firing two of our
cannon a little over their heads; after which we continued our courfe, and on Wednefday morning faw forty
or fifty canoes along fhore, feveral of which came off to
us apparently with hoftile intentions, although they
were not above an hundred in number, and but indif-
ferently armed.   One of their chiefs in the largeft of
the canoes, made feveral long fpeeches; and by the
menacing flourifhes of his hepatoo fpear, feemed to bid
us defiance; but feeing us continue inviting them to
trade, they at length came clofe along fide, and he who
had been their orator, taking up a ftone, after pro-
nouncing a few words, gently threw it againft the fide
of the fhip, which apparently was a formal declaration
of war, as they all immediately took up their arms:
but Tabia threatened them with immediate deftruction
if they began to attack us, and affured them of our pacific intentions, and that we only wanted to purchafe
their fifh, at the fame time fhowing them fome pieces
of fine Otahitee cloth, which had more influence upon
them than all his menaces, for they had no apprehen-
fions of danger from our refentment.   They had a large
quantity of cray-fifh and mufcles, which we purchafed;

but

but with more œconomy than we had before practised, as a piece of cloth which we had usually given for a parcel of fish, was on this occasion divided into seven or eight pieces, and exchanged for so many times the quantity we had formerly received; and yet they thought themselves sufficiently paid. The cloth which they received from us, they cut into bits two or three inches square, which they placed in their ears. While they were trading with us, one of them had the boldness to lay hold of some cloaths which had been fastened to a rope, and thrown into the water to soak. These he untied, and put into his own canoe, and though every man in the ship had seen the transaction, and though a party of marines threatened him with their musquets, yet he obstinately persisted in detaining them; and, without any attempt to escape towards the shore, or remove from along side of the ship   Two balls were then fired through the bottom of his canoe, but without any effect, except that he began with great deliberation to stop the leaks which they had made; and though a charge of small shot was soon after fired into his back, he continued repairing his leaks; occasionally putting up one of his hands to rub the flesh where the shot had penetrated. When their canoe was sufficiently repaired, they precipitately removed some distance from us with their booty,

and

and there began to laugh, greatly pleafed with their acquifition and their dexterity.   A four pounder was then fired towards them, upon which they retired to the fhore.   In the evening a double canoe, built after the model of thofe at Otahitee, but carved and decorated according to their own peculiar manner, followed us a long time, the Indians appearing in good humour, and frequently dancing and finging; at length one of them made a long harrangue, which being finifhed, they all began to pelt us with ftones; but feeing us continue regardlefs of their behaviour, they retired.   The next morning, however, the fame canoe purfued and overtook us about nine o'clock; fhe carried a fail of an odd conftruction, which was made from a kind of matting, and of a triangular figure; the hypotheneufe, or broadeft part, being placed at the top of the maft, and ending in a point at the bottom.   One of its angles was marled to the maft, and another to a fpar with which they altered its pofition according to the direction of the wind, by changing it from fide to fide.   The people in this canoe followed us feveral hours, but finding we purfued our courfe, they laughed heartily at our fuppofed cowardice, and approaching nearer, threw feveral ftones on board, fome of which were near doing us mifchief; we then fired a mufquet at them, but it produ-

cing

cing no effect, a great gun was levelled, which made them retire, though by some accident it missed fire.

Friday, Nov. 4, three canoes came along side, and an Indian in one of them threw a spear on board at one of our crew; but they all fled at the discharge of a musquet. In the afternoon we sailed towards an opening, which we discovered in the land, and the same evening came to anchor in seven fathom with good ground; and were soon after surrounded by several armed canoes, which waited until dark, and then retired, threatening to return the next morning; however, about eleven o'clock the same night, we were again surrounded by them; but finding us on the watch, they soon retired. But in the morning about one hundred and fifty men, in sixteen canoes, all armed with spears and stones, again came off apparently with a fixed determination to begin hostilities: they seemed desirous of boarding the ship, but could not agree on the place, frequently removing from one situation to another, and approaching the sides, bows and quarters successively. These movements kept us on our guard in the rain for some time, in which we employed every expedient we could imagine to pacify them; but these served only to increase their temerity. We then fired several muskets, on which they took to their arms, and attempted to come on board, but the difcharge of a four-pounder fuddenly difperfed them.

Shortly after our boats were fent to found the bay and difcover a more convenient anchorage, which they executed, and returned at three in the afternoon, when we weighed and failed nearer in towards the fouthern fhore, anchoring in five fathom, with a foft fandy bottom. The next morning we were vifited by many of the natives, who came in a peaceable manner, bringing large quantities of fifh, cloth, fpears, &c. which they fold us at very moderate prices. In this bay we procured a large fupply of wood, and of excellent water, and alfo healed our fhip and fcrubbed her bottom, which had become very foul; the natives treating us with great hofpitality on fhore at their own habitations.

Thurfday, the 9th of November, being an uncommon clear day, the aftronomers landed to obferve the Tranfit of Mercury; and during the obfervation a large canoe loaded with various commodities for traffick came a-long-fide, and an officer, who then had the command, willing to encourage them to expofe their goods, lowered down a very large piece of Otahitee

cloth,

cloth, more valuable than any they had ever feen; whereupon the Indians in the canoe, perhaps miftaking his intention, but more probably defirous of robbing him of his property, called upon a young active Indian who ftood neareft the cloth, to feize upon it, which he at firft declined; but afterwards taking it in his hands as if for examination, he fuddenly difengaged it from the rope, and was immediately fhot dead by the officer to whom it belonged, and who having always conducted himfelf with the ftricteft probity, was the more irritated by this deviation from it. But had we punifhed every difhoneft attempt with equal feverity, we muft have extirpated the greateft part of the Indians with whom we have had any commerce; for never were people more ignorant or regardlefs of the principles of natural juftice. Immediately after this unhappy mifconduct, the Indians all fled, and feveral days elapfed before we could allure them to renew their commerce with us. On Saturday the boats were difpatched to examine a large river, which they performed, and returned again in the evening. During our ftay here we found great plenty of oyfters and cellery.

Thurfday

Thurſday morning, the 15th, we ſailed from Mercury Bay ſteering N E. towards a group of iſlands
which we paſſed, with many others, continuing our
courſe until Sunday the 19th, when we entered a
fine ſtreight, and came to anchor in twenty-three fathom the ſame evening ; and on Monday we coaſted
along the north ſide of the ſtreight, about three miles
from the ſhore, in twenty one fathom of water.   But
our ſoundings having afterwards regularly decreaſed
to ſix fathom and a half, we anchored in mid-channel
and diſpatched our boats to found a river running
from S. W. and at ſeven o'clock the next morning we
moored our ſhip, amd were ſoon after viſited by three
trading canoes.   Wedneſday the 22d we weighed,
and ſtood up the ſtreight, having regular ſoundings
from ſeven to fifteen fathom, with blue clay at bottom.

On Friday we had a freſh gale at N. W. with thunder and lightning; but the wind changing to S. W.
we left the bay, and on Saturday coaſted to the northward between ſeveral high iſlands and the main, in
twenty-ſix fathom water, and in the evening anchored
in fourteen fathom, and caught near one hundred
bream with our hooks.

The

The following day many canoes, filled with Indians, came along fide, whom we treated in the beft manner, and made them feveral prefents; but they afterwards, as a return for our hofpitality, began to affail us with ftones; we then fired feveral charges of fmall fhot among the aggreffors, and a mufket ball over them; upon which retiring to a little diftance, and thinking themfelves without our reach, they ftopped and defied us to battle; but feveral great fhot being fired near them, they fled towards the fhore.

The next day feveral canoes with Indians vifited us, but they behaving in a hoftile manner were difperfed by the ufual methods. The wind continuing north-wefterly until Wednefday the 29th, and finding we loft way by turning againft it, we bore away for a place which had the appearance of a bay; and the next morning at eleven o'clock we anchored therein, between an ifland and the main, having four fathom and a half of water, and a fine fandy bottom. Our boats were then fent to found, but the pinnace being furrounded by a party of the natives, who refolutely attempted to go on board, the feamen were compelled to fire upon them, by which they were difperfed. At the return of our boats, finding we had brought to

on

on a bank we weighed, and dropping over it, anchored again in ten fathom and a half: immediately after we were furrounded by thirty-three large canoes, containing above three hundred of the natives, all well armed. They traded peaceably with us for a little time; but on a fignal given by one of their chiefs according to a preconcerted plan, they all immediately quitted the fhip, and removing to the buoy attempted to raife our anchor; expecting, as we fuppofed, that the fhip would afterwards drift on fhore. When they were pulling at our buoy, we fired two or three fhot a little befide them; put perfifting in their attempt, we wounded one of their moft active leaders in the arm and fide, and alfo fired a four-pound ball a little above their heads, on which they not only difperfed, but feveral returned and traded with us peaceably.

In the afternoon captain Cook, with feveral gentlemen, attended by a party of marines, landed on one of the iflands, and incautioufly fuffered themfelves to be furrounded by a great body of Indians, a party of them at the fame time marching down to the boat to cut off their retreat. Thefe motions being immediately feen on board the fhip, a fpring was put on her cables, and a broadfide brought to bear on the ifland,

and

and feveral great fhot fired a little over them: our
people on the ifland were, at this time, feparated in
fmall parties, none confifting of more than three or
four, and fo clofely befet that they found it impoffible
to ufe their arms; and the number of their enemies
was fo unequal, that they every minute expected death.
In the confternation and diforder occafioned by their
dangerous fituation, feveral mufquets were confufedly
difcharged, but fortunately they did no mifchief. The
natives were, however greatly terrified by the paffing
of our cannon balls a little above their heads, and immediately difperfed, at a time when they might with
the greateft facility have deftroyed every one of our
people on fhore. Soon after efcaping this danger we
were vifited by feveral canoes with Indians, who traded
in a peaceable manner. The following day we landed
on an ifland at the weft-fide of the bay, where we
found good water and cellery in great plenty; and alfo
a town where we drew our nets, but with very bad
fuccefs, though the Indians at the fame time caught
large quantities. Their fuccefs was occafioned by
watching the approach of the fifh who came in large
fhoals; together with a difference in the form of their
feines, which were two or three fathoms in depth, and
of proportionable length.

N

Soon

Soon after the difpute on fhore feveral feamen paffing though a plantation of the natives, took from it
a few potatoes, for which they were feverely chaftifed
by the captain ; but they alledged in their juftification
that they had only done what he himfelf and all the
officers had often practifed, and the captain being irritated at this reply, ordered three of them to be con-
fined and punifhed for feveral days fucceffively.

Monday the 4th of December we failed from the
Bay of Iflands, and it being low water, on croffing the
bar we founded in two fathom three quarters, the wind
being from the fouth.   On Wednefday the 6th, coafting by the land, at ten o'clock in the evening it fell
calm, and a ftrong tide flowing at that time, it carried
us, notwithftanding all our endeavours, within twenty
yards of the fhore, which was crowded by the natives, flourifhing their weapons, exulting at our dangers, and expecting us for their prey: but at the in-
ftant when our prefervation appeared hopelefs, a gentle
breeze began from the fhore, and the current of an eddy
at the fame time, turning the head of our fhip from the
land, we happily efcaped from the dangers with which
we had been threatened.   The wind having frefh-
ened about eleven o'clock the fame night, we ftruck
                                                violently

violently againſt a ſunken rock, but happily fell off without any conſiderable damage. In the day time we had obſerved ſeveral breakings in the water near this place, but concluded them to have been occaſioned by the reſpiration of a grampus which we had ſeen a little before.

From the 7th we continued ſailing along the coaſt north-weſterly until the 25th, when we diſcovered the Iſland of Three Kings: in this interval we had experienced a conſtant ſucceſſion of violent gales which greatly damaged our ſails and rigging, and at a time when our canvaſs, and even twine were nearly expended.

Sunday the 31ſt of December at noon, we ſaw Taſman's North Cape, bearing N. N. E. and diſtant four leagues and a half: having paſſed this cape, which is the moſt northern extremity of New Zealand, we altered our courſe to the ſouthward, ſailing along the oppoſite, or eaſt-ſide, towards Murderers Bay, where we propoſed to ſupply ourſelves with wood and water. On Friday the 12th of January, 1760, being in latitude 38° 10, we diſcovered a remarkable peak nearly equal in heigth to that of Teneriffe, which was

covered

covered at its summit with snow. On Monday the
15th in the morning we discovered a bay, about eleven leagues to the S. S. W. and sailed towards it; but
a little after, being two miles from the shore, we were
nearly driven upon a ledge of sunken rocks, which
extend about a mile and an half from the land: but
it being almost calm we hoisted out our boats, and
towed the ship without danger.   We then sent the pinnace to examine a small cove before us, but soon after
recalled her on seeing the natives launch and arm
their canoes.   In sailing towards the bay, we observed
an Indian town, where the inhabitants, by waving their
hands almost incessantly, seemed to invite us to land.
In passing the point of the bay we saw an armed cen-
tinel on duty, who was twice afterwards relieved.
About noon we anchored, and were soon after visited
by many of the natives in their canoes ; but none of
them would venture on board, except an old man, who
was apparently of some distinction among them ; but
in attempting to climb up the ship's side, he was several times forcibly with-held by his countrymen.   At
length, however, he came on board, and Tobia joining noses with him according to the custom of New
Zealand, their apprehensions were thereby removed,
and beginning a loud laugh they immediately came

up

up the fide without the leaft conftraint of timidity. As we paffed the town an old Indian, in a fingular kind of habit, came down to the water fide, attended by feveral of his countrymen, and there performed fome myfterious rites, with a matt and feathers, &c.

Tuefday the 16th, as we prepared to careen our fhip, feveral Indians in canoes came along fide with fifh for fale, which they offered to the deputy-purfer; but on his giving them the ftipulated price, they fuddenly withdrew their fifh, and would have killed him with their hepatoos, had he not precipitately efcaped. This infidious attempt being reprefented to captain Cooke, he feized a fowling-piece, ready loaded with duck fhot, and fired at the aggreffor, who being almoft directly under him, received the charge in his knee, which was thereby fhattered in pieces, a few fcattering fhot likewife paffed through his great toe. His wounds producing a plentiful hemorrhage, he bathed them in falt water, and the pain being acute, he angrily threw the fifh which he had fold, and for which he had been paid, into the fea. The Indians who were in the other canoes, did not appear furprized either at the report of the gun or the wounds it had made, though they all paddled round and examined

them:

them: nor did the wounded Indian retire, but wrapping himfelf up in mats he continued about the fhip feveral hours. A little before this tranfaction, two of thefe Indians being prevented from coming on board by the mafter, who thought there were more on the deck than could be prudently admitted, they immediately drew their fpears to affault him, and force admittance, and nothing but actual violence could drive them back to their canoes.

The fame afternoon the captain, with feveral gentlemen, went in the pinnace to the other fide of the Bay, where they met feveral Indians, who were employed in fifhing. They had feveral bafkets in their canoes, which we examined; and, to our great furprize, found in them feveral limbs, and other parts of human bodies, which had been roafted, and of which it was evident they had lately eaten by the marks of their teeth, which we difcovered in the flefh, and which appeared to have been recently gnawed and torn. We had been before affured, that the inhabitants of New Zealand were cannibals from their own concurrent teftimonies in many different places, but had never occular demonftration of the fact until this time.

When

When we enquired of thefe people, how this human fleſh came into their poffeffion, they told us that five or fix days before a canoe, containing ten men, with two women, had been driven into their bay from a different diſtrict, and that they had attacked and killed them all, excepting one woman, who, in attempting to fwim, had been drowned; and that their bodies were afterwards divided among them, of which the fleſh we had feen was a part. Perhaps they thought, like a celebrated philofopher, that it was as well to feed on the bodies of their enemies, (for by their own accounts they eat no other) as to leave them to be devoured by crows. It is however certain they had no belief of any turpitude in this practice, becaufe they were not aſhamed of it; but, on the contrary, when we took up an arm for examination, they imagined us to be defirous of the fame kind of food, and with great good-nature promifed that they would the next day fpare a human head ready roafted, if we would come or fend to fetch it. Some gentlemen, who never left their own homes, have ventured, on the ftrength of fpeculative reafoning, to queftion the veracity of thofe travellers who have publiſhed accounts of cannibals in Africa and America; treating as falfehoods every relation, which, from their ignorance of human nature, appears to them improba-

ble;

ble: but let them not indulge the fame freedom on this occafion; the fact will be too well attefted to be rendered doubtful by their vifionary impertinent objections.

While we were converfing with our cannibals, we obferved fomething on fhore roafting after the manner practifed by the inhabitants of George's Ifland, which they told us was a young dog; but fufpecting it to be human flefh, we were going to open the oven, when we faw the hair and entrails of a dog, which fatisfied us concerning the truth of their account.

Wednefday, having finifhed careening our fhip, we began to wood and water; but in going to that part of the bay where we had difcovered the bafkets of human flefh, we found the body of a woman floating on the water, which we fuppofed to be the fame that had been drowned in attempting to efcape by fwimming, as before related; but fhe was foon after claimed by an Indian, who told us fhe was his fifter, and having died had been funk in the fea, according ro the cuftom of their tribe; a cuftom which, however, is peculiar to the inhabitants of this bay.

In this part of New Zealand we faw many towns, whofe inhabitants had either fled or been exterminated; fome of them appeared to have been deferted or uninhabited four or five years, being overgrown with fhrubs and high grafs. On a fmall ifland, lying S. E. from the place where we anchored, was one of thefe deferted towns, moft agreeably fituated, and confifting of about eighteen houfes, placed in a circular form; it was furrounded and defended by a wall curioufly conftructed, by driving two rows of long ftakes or fpars into the ground, at convenient diftances, and afterwards filling the intermediate fpace with what we called broom-ftuff, being a fmall kind of brufh, made into bundles like faggots, and placed on end, in double rows, fupported by others lying parallel with the ground: in this manner the wall is raifed fix or feven feet in height, and, notwithftanding the fimplicity of its ftructure, it is not eafily broken or deftroyed, efpecially when guarded by men, who fight not only to preferve freedom and property, but their own bodies from being cruelly butchered and eaten.

At a little diftance from this town we faw the remains of a more regular fortification, fituated on a high hill, near a pleafant bay. The hill itfelf was almoft inacceffible,

fible,

fible, and on its top was a level flat, large enough for a town, which was furrounded by a fence made from fpars two feet in circumference, drove deep into the earth, and about twenty feet in height: thefe were placed in contact with each other, and without them was a ditch about ten feet in breadth : within the fence were feveral large refervoirs for water, and ftages adjoining to the fpars for fupporting thefe who were placed to guard the town, which appeared to have been fpacious enough to contain two or three hundred houfes, though none were then remaining. The fides of the hill in every part were fo fteep, that nobody could afcend them, except by crawling on his hands and knees.

At the bottom of this hill we obferved the ruins of a town, which had belonged to the proprietors of this caftle, and which was the place of their common refidence ; for, befides their town, the natives have always a feparate fort or ftrong hold, which ferves them for a place of retreat, and a magazine for fecuring their dried fifh, fern root, and other provifions; and, to prevent its being taken by furprize, they always leave a fufficient number of armed men therein, and thither they all retreat upon an alarm; always keeping in

readinefs

readinefs a fufficient quantity of water in refervoirs, and regular piles of fpears and ftones difperfed along the ftage adjoining to the fence; the height of thefe ftages being fitted to afford thofe on guard fufficient fhelter behind the fence, and fo much elevation, as not to be impeded by it in flinging their ftones or ufing their fpears, &c.

Some of thefe caftles, which have not the advantages of an elevated fituation, to fupply thofe defects are furrounded by two or three wide ditches, with a draw-bridge, which, though fimple in its ftructure, is capable of anfwering every purpofe: and within thefe ditches is a fence, made from fpars fixed in the earth after the manner of that which was laft defcribed, but with this difference, that they incline inwardly; a circumftance which we thought favourable to the befiegers; but, on communicating this opinion to one of their chiefs, he affured us of the contrary; obferving, that if the fpars fhould be pointed or inclined outwardly towards the enemy, that inclination would afford the affailants an opportunity of fheltering themfelves under their points, from which it might be impoffible to diflodge them; and that they would there be able to dig fubterraneous paffages into the caftle. The fame

O 2 chief

chief told us that thefe ftrong holds were never taken, unlefs by furprize ; or when the enemy, being mafters of the field, converted the fiege into a blockade, and de- priving them of all external fubfiftence, occafioned a famine within ; and when this happens, the befieged, having no hope of foreign aid, all their friends and countrymen being fhut up in the fame caftle, are com- pelled either to perifh with hunger, or fally out and meet the fpears of their enemies. And hence a deci- five victory or conqueft occafions the entire depopula- tion of that diftrict, which was inhabited by the van- quifhed ; all thofe who are killed or taken prifoners be- ing devoured by their enemies. I would however hope, for the honour of mankind, that this favage practice has been produced among them only from the groffeft depravation of human nature; for in its pri- mitive ftate I fhould be forry to believe it would feel no repugnance at a meal, which brutes will not make on the bodies of their own fpecies.

Having procured a fufficient fupply of wood and water, on the 6th of February, 1770, the wind being northerly, we left Charlotte Sound, failing along the coaft to the eaftward: but it falling calm towards evening, we anchored about three quarters of a mile

from

from the Hippa in ten fathoms of water, and fent our boats a fifhing. The next morning we made fail, but the tide foon after carried us rapidly towards a clufter of rocks, projecting from an ifland at a fmall diftance, and the wind failing, our fituation became juftly alarming. At this time one of the principal officers propofed endeavouring to crofs the tide, and gain a paffage between two iflands; and this gentleman's ftation made his propofal, though impracticable, of fo much importance at this critical feafon, that the captain, who was about to give orders of a different kind, became irrefolute; and during the difpute which this contrariety of opinion occafioned, we were carried fo near the rocks that our prefervation appeared almoft impoffible; and at this critical juncture we could only let go our beft bower, which we inftantly did, with all fail ftanding, in feventy five fathom; and after veering out a hundred and fixty fathoms of cable, we found the fhip brought up by her anchor, to our great joy. But had this expedient failed, fhe muft have been irrecoverably loft, and all her crew left either to build a veffel to tranfport themfelves to the Eaft-Indies; or, if that fhould be impracticable, to pafs their lives in New Zealand, if they fhould be able to defend themfelves from the jaws of cannibals.

It

It ought to be remarked, that Tafman, when he vifited Murderers Bay, imagined that there muft be a ftreight running through the country to the oppofite fhore; and this he did from obferving that the flood-tide ran in ftrong from S. E. and therefore while lying in Charlotte Sound, we had afcended the top of a neighbouring mountain, to fee if we could obferve the appearance of a ftreight or paffage, which we there difcovered, and upon enquiring of the natives concerning it, they told us it was navigable to the other fide of the country; and that the fouthern divifion of New Zealand might be failed round in one of their canoes in four days time. This information determined us to make the experiment; and accordingly we ftood toward the ftreight, which we found, and paffed the next day, near the middle of the channel; and, though the land was vifible on each fide, yet, to prevent the poffibility of a deception, after paffing the ftreight, we ftood to the northward until we made Cape Turnagain, which we did on Friday noon: and having thus determined the reality of the ftreight, we altered our courfe to the fouthward, refolving to fail round the other divifion of New Zealand. We continued our courfe, expecting to find the land incline to the weftward, but were difappointed in our expectation:

tation: indeed we obferved fomething like the appearance of a paffage fome leagues fouth from the ftreights,
but the whole company were divided in opinion about
the matter; though from the reports of the Indians,
it is not improbable that there was a paffage navigable for their canoes, if not for veffels of burthen. We
perfifted in our defign of difcovering whether the
fouthern divifion of New Zealand was an ifland or
continent, but were frequently oppofed in our courfe
by heavy winds from the fouth, in one of which, on
the 26th of February, our forefail was irreparably
torn in pieces, and our main topfail divided afunder;
and the gale continuing violent for feveral days after
tompelled us to lie to. The tempeftuous feafon ad-
vancing faft, and the air being very cold, we began
to defpair of a fouthern paffage, having been more
than a month employed on a difcovery which might
have been completed with favourable winds in a few
days.

On the 9th of March, at four in the morning, after having complained of the want of wind all night,
we were furprifed to find a ledge of rocks about half
a mile forwards, and extending a-crofs both our bows.
We had then abundant reafon to rejoice at the provi-
dential

dential calm the preceding night, as a few minutes
favourable wind would have occafioned our certain deftruction. Thefe rocks lie S. E. from the fouthern
extreme of New Zealand, and at the diftance of twenty miles.

On the 10th we doubled the Southern Cape in latitude 47° 39′ S. and longitude 191° 35′ W. and again
ftood to the northward on the weft fide, with a favourable wind; intending to return to Charlotte Sound,
and replenifh our ftores of wood and water, if no convenient place was difcovered nearer. The land on this
part of the coaft afforded a moft dreary profpect, and
confifted of very high mountains covered with fnow,
and falling by the fteepeft defcent immediately into the
fea, without the fmalleft beach or landing-place. Nor
could we any where difcover the fmalleft appearance
of a human inhabitant.

On Monday the 26th of March, in latitude 40° 32′,
being thirty-three miles north from Charlotte Sound, we
ftood into a deep bay or found, having iflands on both
fides, and thirty fix fathom of water at one mile diftance from fhore; and fteering in S. by W. we anchored in Admiralty Bay on the left fide in eleven fathom
muddy

muddy ground; and mooring with the ftream-anchor, began to fupply our ftock of wood and water. We found this place intirely uninhabited, and but badly fheltered from eafterly winds. But it afforded plenty of wood and water, as well as of fifh, of which we caught more than fufficient for our confumption with hooks. We difcovered an old houfe by the fide of a mountain, at a little diftance from the bay, and the wreck of an old canoe lying in a cove contiguous to it. We had now paffed near fix months on the coaft of New Zealand, had furveyed it on every fide, and, which was not before known, had difcovered to be an ifland near three hundred leagues in length, and inhabited by cannibals, habituated to the carnage of war from infancy, and of all mankind the moft fearlefs and infenfible of dangers.

It deferves to be remarked, that the people of New Zealand fpoke the language of Otahitee with but very little difference, not fo much as is found between many counties in England; a circumftance of the moft extraordinary kind, and which muft neceffarily lead us to conclude, that one of thefe places was originally peopled from the other, though they are at near two thoufand miles diftance; and nothing but the ocean in-

P   tervenes,

tervenes, which we fhould hardly believe they could navigate fo far in canoes, the only veffels that they appear to have ever poffeffed ; for as there is no natural relation between founds and the ideas they are made to convey by fpeaking ; fo it muft be evident, that neither the fuggeftions of reafon or of nature, would ever lead two diftinct, feparate people, having no communication with each other, to affix the fame meaning to the fame words, and employ them as the medium of communication. It muft, therefore, be inferred, that the inhabitants of one of thefe iflands originally migrated from the other, though, upon comparing the manners, drefs, arms, &c. of the people of Otahitee with thofe of New Zealand, as far as they have fallen under our obfervation, we fhall find them difagree in feveral important particulars, but in feveral others they have apparent analogy.

The New Zealanders not only neglect circumcifion, but, on the contrary, confider the prepuce as fo neceffary, that they commonly tie its forwards with a ligature, to cover the glans penis, and preferve its fenfibility, as they themfelves alledge. They mark their bodies in fpiral circles, by introducing blue paint under the fkin after it has been punctured according to the

manner

manner of Otahitee; they have likewife beards and
long hair, which they tie at the top of the head, like
the natives of Otahitee.   They differ, however, in complection, being much browner than thofe of George's
Ifland, though both feem to agree in their propenfities
to knavery; but in martial courage the new Zealanders are much fuperior; and indeed it is impoffible to
fee, without aftonifhment, the degree of madnefs to
which they will elevate themfelves even in their ha-
rangues, that are preparatory to a feigned battle.

Their cloaths are made from the fibres of a fpecies of
filk grafs, wove by knotting or tying the woof together
in lines, commonly about a quarter of an inch diftant; and are curioufly embroidered at the corners and
edges with black and brown figures, and fringed with
dogs hair; and when worn are tied over the fhoulders
with ftrings, and depend below the loins.   They likewife wear belts made from a kind of ftrong grafs braided together.

Like the people of George's Ifland, they never boil
their meat, but always bake it in fubterraneous ovens.
Their weapons are the Patty Petow, which is made
either of wood, bone, or ftone, and confifts of a handle

P 2   joined

joined to a broad flat two edged blade.   The battle axe, which is made from a fpecies of very hard, heavy wood, and has a very long handle. They have likewife wooden fpears, with hair taffels near their points, which are fometimes wood, and at others the fpear of the fting ray-fifh.   It is remarkable, however, that, notwithftanding the natives of Otahitee ufe bows and arrows with great dexterity, thofe of New Zealand were wholly un-acquainted with them, until we firft taught them their ufe: a circumftance which renders it probable that the migration was from New Zealand to George's Ifland, and that the inhabitants of the latter difcovered the ufe of bows by fome accident, after their feparation; as it cannot be fuppofed the New Zealanders would have loft fo beneficial an acquifition, if they had ever been ac-quainted with it.   Their trumpets are near two feet in length, having a large broad flat belly or concavity, with a large hole about the middle; thefe produce a fhrill hoarfe found.   They commonly wear a fmall wooden whiftle tied about the neck, which is open at both ends, and has two other perforations or holes. Their combs are made from bone or wood, and have very long coarfe teeth. Many of them wear an image carved from a greenifh ftone, made into an odd half human fi-gure, which is tied about the neck.   They likewife wear

fmall

fmall images of wood or flone, and fometimes the teeth of a deceafed relation, which depend from their ears. Their axes and fifh-hooks are like thofe of Otahitee.

On the 31ft of March we left Admiralty Bay, and failed fouth-wefterly, towards New Holland, taking our departure from a point which we named Cape Farewell. By inftructions, opened here, we were directed to return home By Cape Hormor, and to ftop at the Eaft Indies, if neceffary.

April the 18th, towards the evening, judging ourfelves near the land, we handed topfails; and at night lying-to we founded with one hundred and thirty fathom of line, but found no ground. The next morning we made fail, and an hour after difcovered the coaft of New Holland, rifing very high between N. E. by N. and W. by S. and diftant eight leagues, being in latitude 37° 50' S. and longitude 31° 00' W. from Cape Farewell. We then fteered N. N. E. along fhore, at the diftance of four leagues. Friday the 20th, in the morning we faw the appearance of an ifland at N. N. W. On Saturday we faw a fmoke on fhore, and afterwards a high hill, which we named Cape Dromedary, from its likenefs to the back of that animal.

This

This cape is in latitude 36° 21′ S. and longitude 150°
28′ E. variation 10° 42′ Eaſt.   In the afternoon we ſaw
two ſmall iſlands, bearing W. by S. diſtant two leagues.

On· Sunday we ſaw ſeveral of the natives kindling
fires along the ſhore ; the land extending a little to the
eaſtward of north, we ſteered along the coaſt northward-
ly, intending to anchor in the firſt bay.   Friday afternoon we endeavoured to land with our boat, but found
the ſurf running too high. Saturday morning, the 28th,
we diſcovered a bay at N. by E. and ſtood towards it,
ſending the pinnace forwards to ſound; and at half
after one in the afternoon we anchored in ſix fathom
and a half, ſandy ground.   But on attempting to land
in our boats, a few of the natives advanced towards the
ſhore, and two of them, armed with ſhields and ſpears,
reſolutely oppoſed our diſembarkation, until being
wounded by our ſhot, and unſupported by any of their
countrymen, they retreated ſlowly to their houſes within the buſhes, but conſtantly faced us the whole way.
This they did to gain time for their wives to remove
themſelves and children, with their domeſtic and culi-
nary utenſils farther into the woods, and when this
was done they haſtily retreated themſelves.

Their

Their huts were wretchedly built, and but little better than thofe belonging to the inhabitants of Terra del Fuego, as they confifted of nothing more than pieces of the bark of trees loofely fpread over a few crofs fpars, about four feet above the ground. The inhabitants were intirely naked and black, but they differed from the negroes of Africa in having long ftrait hair inftead of wool on their heads. On their breafts we obferved rude figures of men, darts, &c. done with a kind of white paint; which was alfo daubed irregularly on other parts of their bodies. Their arms or weapons, which afterwards fell into our poffeffion, were fpears made of a kind of light wood, and acutely pointed with bones barbed on different fides, to render their wounds more deleterious: in thefe fpears we fometimes difcovered junctures, united by a kind of refinous cement. They had other kinds of fpears for ftriking fifh, which were forked at the points.

Their fhields were oval, about three feet in length, and one in breadth, being concave within, and provided with handles. In fome of them we obferved fmall holes or apertures, defigned to afford a profpect of the movements of their enemies when the fhield is

employed

employed for guarding the head. They have likewife a kind of fwords, made from a very folid compact hard fpecies of wood. In retiring to the woods they left behind two or three canoes of a very fimple ftructure, being made from the bark enclofing one fide or half of the trunk of a tree, which they had tied together at each end by a kind of flexible withy twig, and fpread or feparated in the middle by pieces of wood placed acrofs from fide to fide : thefe canoes were about ten feet in length, and their paddles were about two feet long, and at the blade three inches broad: one of them being held in each hand, they pull themfelves forward with great celerity. But notwithftanding the little value of thefe canoes, they were unwilling to loofe them, and returned foon after our deture, and watching an opportunity conveyed them away to a different place.

The natives apparently fubfift chiefly on fifh, of which there is great plenty, efpecially of the fting ray-fifh, weighing between two and three hundred pounds; and as they commonly fwim in fhallow water, they are eafily taken : of thefe and other kinds we caught great quantities.

The

The foil of New Holland we found to be rocky and fandy in many places, but at this bay the adjacent country appeared level, moderately elevated, and well covered with trees, having but few fhrubs intermixed to obftruct the profpect. On the furface of the earth we obferved feveral kinds of grafs growing plentifully, and in fome places luxuriantly. Among the trees we could diftinguifh but five kinds, or rather fpecies; of which the moft common is that yielding the fanguis draconis, or dragon's blood: the next is the etoe tree of Otahitee; the cabbage-tree, and two others, which we cut for fire-wood.

We obferved the dung of a quadruped, probably of the fame fpecies with thofe we afterwards killed at Endeavour River. Our greyhound likewife purfued a fmall animal, but ftaked himfelf in the chace without overtaking it. Crows and cockatoos we obferved in great numbers; together with a very beautiful bird of the lory kind, which we called loryquet. Captain Cooke, with a party, made an incurfion into the country, hoping for an opportunity of taking fome of the natives, intending to cloath and make them prefents, and afterwards fend them back to their friends; ex-pecting that fuch a proof of our pacific intentions

Q

would

would be fufficient to engage them to pay us a vifit,
and enter into fome commerce and traffic ; but they
were not fortunate enough to difcover any of them;
however, they left fome cloaths, combs, garters, look-
ing-glaffes, knives, &c. in an empty hut which had
been lately deferted : but thefe prefents were never
carried away during our continuance in this part of
the country, though we had reafon to believe the
place had been vifited feveral times after by the
natives.

A few days after two officers with a party of men
went in a boat to the head of the bay to fifh, where
they found feveral of the natives, who fingled out as
many men from among themfelves as they had
counted in the boat, and thefe came down to the
water's edge (their countrymen throwing down their
arms and retiring a good diftance) and there they
challenged us to battle ; but this being refufed, they
felected two only, out of their number, and challenged as many of us to fight them, the others retiring to avoid any fufpicion of treachery : but this of-
fer being likewife rejected, they all retired ; but foon
after feveral others came to the fhore, and an officer
fired a mufket loaded with a ball into a tree at fome

distance,

distance, that he might let them fee how far it would carry; and being much pleafed at the fight, they defired him, by figns, to let them fee another difcharge, which he did, and they foon after retired apparently well pleafed. The officers then determining to return by land through the woods, difpatched the boats forwards, but they had not proceeded above two miles on their way, before they were overtaken by two and twenty of the natives, all armed, who followed clofe at their heels, but ftopped whenever the officers faced them, and retired if they began to advance towards them, but again followed them when they proceeded on their way to the place where the boat had been directed to wait: in this manner they continued their return, until they came near the place where a part of our crew was employed in cutting wood, when they were joined by feveral other gentlemen who had been fhooting, and one of them propofed a fcheme to entrap fome of the Indians, which had near proved fatal. The defign was to advance as near to the natives as they would permit, without retiring; and then feigning a fright, to turn fuddenly and run from them, expecting in this manner to decoy them in a purfuit which might afford the working parties an opportunity of furrounding and taking fome of them:

but

but whether the Indians fufpected the artifice or not, the gentlemen had not ran above twelve yards after their pretended fright, before the natives, giving loud fhrieks, advanced haftily, and threw their fpears at them with great force. One of the gentlemen who was near-eft, hearing their cry, fuddenly turned his head, and feeing the fpears in their flight, had fcarce fufficient time to fave himfelf behind a tree, though but at a few feet diftance: one of the fpears entered the ground which he had quitted, and another pierced deep into the tree behind which he had fheltered himfelf. Many others fell in different places, one fticking faft in the branch of a tree above the head of a gentleman who had ran the fartheft from them, and who was then at more than fifty yards diftance; another paffed between his legs into the ground. After this attack, they all precipitately retired to the woods; and we, collecting their fpears, returned with them to our fhip. And having procured a fufficient fupply of wood and water, on Sunday the 6th of Auguft, in the morning, we failed from the bay, which we named Sting-ray Bay, from the great quantity of thofe fifh which it contained. It is in latitude 34° 00′, and longitude 209° 13 W. From thence we failed north eafterly along the coaft a few leagues from the fhore, that we might be able to

furvey

furvey the land, and occafionally procure fupplies of
wood and water, or endeavour to eftablifh a traffic
with the natives; as we could not expect to find a paffage into the Indian fea, before we fhould arrive within
nine or ten degrees of latitude from the equator. After
paffing within feveral fmall iflands on the 16th of
May, being in latitude 27° 46′ S. and longitude 2° 18′
E. from Sting ray Bay, we difcovered breakers on the
larboard bow, extending to the eaftward; and immediately after we changed our courfe farther from
fhore, until eight o'clock in the evening, when we
hove to in fixty feven fathom of water.   In the morning we again faw breakers on the larboard bow; and
at feven o'clock in the evening faw another ledge of
breakers at N. W. by W. and founded in one
hundred and thirty-five fathom.   We continued
ftanding to the northward until the 20th, when the land
appeared as terminating in a point at N. W. and fteering towards it, we faw a ledge of breakers extending
feveral miles; we had then fixteen fathom of water, but
it gradually diminifhed to feven and a half, and afterwards encreafed to 11 fathom, being then in latitude
24° 26′ S.   On the 21ft we paffed over the end of a
fhoal, and obferved the land extend wefterly. The night
being calm, we found a current fetting S. W. one knot

and

and a half per hour.   The next evening, being calm,
we anchored in eight fathom, and found, that the tide
did not rife or fall above two feet.   Coafting along
fhore the 23d, we opened a large bay, and at night anchored in it in five fathom.   This was in latitude 24°
00′ S.   A ledge of breakers extends from its northern
extremity or point.   The 24th we made fail, coafting
along fhore; being frequently furrounded with fhoals
and fmall iflands.   On the 25th we caught feveral fifh
of the fnapper kind.   The 26th we anchored in thirteen
fathom water, and found the tide fall feven feet, ebbing
to the eaftward.   The next morning we made fail, and
paffed between a great many iflands, as we did on the
27th, keeping our boats forwards to found.   On the
29th we anchored in a bay in latitude 22° 6′ S.   Here
we continued until the 31ft, when we failed to the
N. W. having a chain of iflands, rocks and fhoals on
our right, the branches of trees on the iflands frequently extending acrofs almoft to the main land.

On the 10th of June we anchored in a bay in lat.
16° 10′ S. and the next morning continued our courfe
north-wefterly: at nine we paffed over a bed of rocks,
fhoaling our water from twenty-one to eight fathom;
and foon after the fhip ftruck on the rocks, and continued

tinued faft upon them. We then handed our fails with the utmoft hafte, and hoifted out our boats, when after founding round the fhip, we found her lying on a reef of rocks running to the N. W. We then ftruck our yards and top mafts, and carried an anchor to the fouthward, and the fhip ftriking very hard, we carried another to the S. W. The next morning all our iron and ftone-ballaft, firewood, fpare ftores, and fix of our great guns were thrown overboard, together with all our water, and many of our water-cafks: and finding the fhip continue to leak very faft, we cut off the heels of our fpare fopmafts, that the foremaft pumps might be worked. At noon the fhip inclined greatly to the ftarboard fide, and we therefore carried the fmall bower to the weftward, lafhed blocks to both bower cables, reeved hawzers, and hove tort upon all five anchors. At four it was low water, and the fhip in feveral places was found lying dry upon the rocks: though we obferved the whole rife of the tide did not exceed four feet. At half paft nine the fhip righted, and at ten we hove her afloat, and letting go the ftream cable and fmall bower, (which were both loft) we brought the beft bower and coafting anchors forward. And notwithftanding we had all the time kept our pumps conftantly employed, the water in the

fhip

ſhip continually increaſed, and we expected either to
ſink at our anchors, or be compelled to warp ourſelves
again upon the rocks, unleſs a breeze ſhould ſpring
up and enable us to reach the ſhore, where we might
ſave ſo much of the wreck as would enable us to
build a ſmall bark to convey ourſelves to ſome European ſettlement in the Eaſt Indies. But when ſur-
rounded with theſe unfavourable proſpects, we happily
found means to fother our ſhip in a manner which ſo
far ſtopped her leaks, that we were able to keep them
under with a ſingle pump; and a favourable wind
ſoon after ariſing, we ſailed in towards the main land,
ſending our boats forward in ſearch of a harbour,
which they fortunately diſcovered at N. W. two or three
leagues diſtant; and on the 14th at nine in the morning we anchored a little without it; finding the paſſage ſo narrow, that it would be neceſſary to lay buoys
along the channel for our direction. But about this
time, the wind which had happily ceaſed while we lay
on the rocks, began to blow ſo hard that we were unable to warp in until the 18th, when, notwithſtand-
ing our precaution, we grounded twice in the paſſage. At length, however, we conveyed the ſhip to
the ſide of a ſteep bank on the north ſide of a river;
and having there ſecured her, we erected tents on

ſhore,

fhore to receive the fick, together with our provifions, and immediately began to unload, that we might lay the fhip on the bank, and there examine and repair her leaks; this we effected by the 22d, and upon examination found four of her planks cut through by the rocks, and a large piece of a rock fticking faft in a hole through the bottom, which had in a great meafure excluded the water, and thereby faved us from finking; feveral more of her ftreaks were much damaged, and a confiderable part of her fheathing and falfe keel beaten off. Having fufficiently repaired the fhip, we lafhed many fpars and cafks under her bottom, that we might heave her afloat, but found it neceffary to wait feveral days until the fpring tides fhould come to our affiftance; and in the mean time we fent the boats to fearch for another paffage, which they found, and returned on the 3d of July, and on the 4th, the fhip being afloat, was warped to a bank on the fouth fide of the river, that we might there examine her aftern, but finding fhe had fuffered no confiderable damage in that part, we returned to our former fituation, where we began to replace our rigging, and take our ftores on board; and the mafter

R

going

going again in fearch of a paffage, faw a great number of tortoifes, of which he caught three, each weighing three hundred pounds.

July the 18th we had nearly refitted for fea; and
the natives of the country, after various expedients had
been employed to convince them of our benevolent intentions, now began to vifit us: we found them very
low of ftature, commonly not more than five feet in
height, fmall and flender in fhape, but very active.
Many of them had flat nofes, thick lips, and bandy
legs, like the negroes of Guinea. They were ignorant,
poor, and deftitute, not only of the conveniencies, but
of many of the neceffaries of life. They were ftrangers to bread, and to every thing which can be confidered as a fubftitute for it; nor would they eat of it
when we gave it to them. They were naked and flo-
venly, fubfifting moftly on fifh, which they roaft on
wooden fpits ftuck into the earth before a fire. We
faw none of their women; but the men had each a
hole made through the feptum nafi, or divifion of the
noftrils, in which a bone five or fix inches in length
was inferted, and worn as an ornament; and however
ludi-

ludicrous it might appear, it is but juſt to obſerve, that many of our European ornaments have no more relation to natural fitneſs or utility, than this unexpenſive one which the poor ignorant New Hollanders have invented. Beſides the bones in their noſes, they wear others of equal length in their ears; which though not ſo brilliant as the ornaments that depend from the ears of the fair ſex in civilized countries, may be as uſeful and proper.

On the 19th of June ſeveral of the natives went to the place where our tents had ſtood, but from which every thing was removed, except a markee, and a part of our ſtores, and taking each a brand of fire, placed them in the graſs, and employed every expedient to kindle and ſpread the flame on every ſide; and ſo ſucceſsful were they in this attempt, that we with great difficulty ſaved our fiſhing-nets and linen, which were ſpread on the ground, from this ſudden conflagration. Captain Cooke wounded ſeveral of them while executing this miſchievous plan, upon which they retired to the woods, but a few hours after they returned peaceably.

We

We continued waiting either for a favourable wind or a calm, until the 4th of Auguſt, when we warped out of the river, which we named Endeavour River, and which is in latitude $15°26'$S. and longitude $216°02'$ W. from thence ſailing into the offing, we came to an anchor in fifteen fathom; and the wind blowing freſh from S. E. we continued here until the 6th, when at two o'clock P. M. we made ſail, ſtanding N. E. by E. and half paſt four we ſaw a ſmall ſandy iſland on a ſhoal, at N. E. by N. diſtant four miles, with breakers forwards, and on the weather bow; we then ſtood off and on, until the boats having ſounded and diſcovered not more than ſix feet of water on the neareſt part of the ſhoal, we immediately anchored with our beſt bower, veering out the whole cable; and the wind blowing very freſh at low water, we endeavoured to diſcover a ſafe paſſage from the maſt head, but to no purpoſe. At ſeven in the evening we found the ſhip drifting, and immediately let go another anchor, and ſtruck our topmaſts and yards. Here we continued until the 10th, when the weather becoming moderate, we made ſail, and ſtood towards a paſſage which the maſter had diſcovered; ſteering between the iſland-ſhoals and the main land in ſeventeen fathom. The

next

next day we difcovered low land with breakers at N. W.
and came to anchor in five fathom, when the captain
went in the pinnace to examine the appearance of a paffage to the eaftward, and the mafter to the fouthward,
to examine a paffage between feveral low iflands and the
main land; and on Sunday noon he returned, having
found between five and eight fathom of water in the
channel.

Monday the 13th, at eleven o'clock, we paffed to
the northward of two reefs and of fix iflands, bearing
S. E. at the diftance of one mile. On the fourteenth we
paffed another fhoal, feven miles weft from Endeavour
River ; and failing north-wefterly on the fixteenth, we
difcovered high land at W. S. W. and foon after a reef
of rocks extending from north to fouth as far as we
could fee. We then ftood farther from fhore ; but it
falling calm at night, the next morning at four o'clock
we faw breakers clofe to the lee bow, and the flood tide
fetting us towards them; at three quarters after five the
fhip was within the furf, and but forty yards from the
rocks, though on founding we could find no ground.
Soon after we difcovered a fmall opening between the
rocks, through which we endeavoured to tow the fhip;

but

but the tide, by changing foon after, fruftrated our defign. On the 17th we again refolved to attempt a paffage through the opening, as the only expedient to preferve the fhip; and accordingly towed her fhort round
W. by S. to the entrance, and from thence S. W. by W.
one-half W. two miles diftance through to the oppofite
fide, the current of the flood tide being ftrong in our
favour. And at four o'clock the fame afternoon, we anchored in nineteen fathom of water, being in latitude 12°
38' and longitude 143° 17' E. Variation 4° 9' E.

On the 18th we made fail, fteering N. W. and foon
after paffed feveral iflands and fhoals; and the fame
evening anchored in thirteen fathom. On the 19th
we failed between a large flat fhoal and the main land.

On Monday the 21ft of Auguft we paffed feveral flats,
and obferved feveral openings in the main land, which
appeared like iflands, fome of them at a great diftance;
and at half paft two in the afternoon, we ftood towards
a paffage, which feemed to extend through the country, and the fame evening anchored about the middle
of it, at the diftance of near a mile from either fhore, in
feven fathom of water, with good ground. Immediately

ately after a party landed from the ship, to examine
the country; and from fmall eminence difcovered the
Indian fea; upon which they fired feveral vollies, and
were anfwered by a general difcharge from the fhip.
We then took poff. ffion of the country, &c. in the name
of his Britannic Majefty; and the next morning weighed anchor, and fteering S. W. by W. failed through the
Strait, which feparates New Holland from New Guinea; and which we now difcovered to be parts of the
fame continent.   Having paffed the ftreight in latitude
10° 36′ S. and longitude 141° 44′, E. we failed along
the fhores of New Guinea; and on the 31ft of Auguft
difcovered Valeh Cape in latitude 8° 25′, S. and longitude 136° 50 E.   The coaft in this part of the country became fo very fhoal, that we found it unfafe to
approach nearer the fhore than five leagues with the
fhip.   But on the 4th of September we landed with
the yawl, expecting to procure a fmall fupply of provifions, fruit, &c. as we had feen cocoa-nut and plain-
tain trees growing in abundance.   The natives, however, affembled at our landing in great numbers, and
began to attack us with their arrows, which were very
long, and fell on every fide, though we were unable
to difcover by what machine or contrivance they were

impelled

impelled or thrown towards us.   We likewife obferved another inftrument of a fingular but unknown con-ftruction, which they frequently employed; and which, after feveral quick revolutions and turnings, always emit-ted a large fmoak, though without any explofion or other effect which we could difcover.

Finding the people of New Guinea unalterably de-termined on hoftilities, and being impatient of return-ing to Europe, we left the coaft; and, to the great joy of the whole company, fteered W. by S. for the Indies. On the 5th we faw a long low ifland, and another on the 6th. The 10th we difcovered the fouth end of Cape Timor, where we would gladly have ftopped for fup-plies, but for an apprehenfion of being detained by the Dutch Government.   This determined us to continue our courfe to the ifland of Sabee, where we anchored in a fmall bay on the 18th. Here we found a Dutch refi-dent or factor, placed to purchafe rice, &c. from the Ra-jas. The ifland produces buffaloes, fmall fheep, poul-try and fruit in abundance, with great quantities of toddy, a kind of fyrup boiled from the juice of palms. The Dutch refident promifed us a fupply of provifions; but contriving feveral unneceffary delays, we imagined

he

he expected a gratuity for affifting us with his good offices; and therefore gave five guineas for a buffalo, which being, as we fuppofed, paid afterwards to him, we, in a little time, were permitted to purchafe as many of thefe animals as we chofe, for a mufquet and bayonet each.

After a ftay of two or three days at Sabee, we failed for Batavia, where we arrived the 9th of October *. At Batavia it was found neceffary to careen and re-fit our fhip; the bottom having been fo much eaten by worms and abraded by rocks, that its thicknefs in many places did not exceed the eight of an inch. And though we had before buried but one man who did not die from fome accidental injury or violence, yet upon our arrival here the crew foon became un-healthy, and our furgeon, with feveral others, died; among whom were Tobia and Tiato, the Indians who had attached themfelves to us at George's Ifland.

After a ftay of near three months at Batavia, we failed for the Cape of Good Hope; but had fcarce

---

* As the courfe from Batavia to Europe is already fufficiently known, the re-maining part of our voyage will be very curforily defcribed.

S

quitted

quitted the land before a putrid dyfentery feized the greateft part of our crew, and raged with fuch violence that not above fix men on board were capable of duty. Of this terrible diforder many of our officers and feamen died, together with Mr. Green the aftronomer, who being infenfible of his danger until feized by a delirium which continued till his death, left the minutes of his obfervations in a ftate of diforder which muft render feveral of them unintelligible.

On our arrival at the Cape, a houfe was immediately hired to receive our fick, who were landed and provided with proper diet and affiftance; and, after procuring fufficient fupplies of water and provifion, we failed to Saint Helena, where we found his majefty's fhip Portland, with twelve Eaft-India fhips, all bound for England.

We failed from St. Helena the 4th of May, in company with this fleet; but parted foon after, and arrived in the Downs on the 15th of July, after near three years abfence, and the lofs of near half of our company.

F I N I S.

Vocabulary of the Language of Otahitee.

A

Aa	A	Ayea.	*A maft.*
	Armpits.	Ayoue	*Smelling.*
Abaremar	*Palm of the hand.*		
Abobo	*Tomorrow.*		**B**
Abobo-durar	*Two days hence.*	Baracee	*The thighs.*
Addie	*A cocoa-nut.*	Boar	*A hog.*
Affarre	*A houfe.*	Bopotarear	*The ear.*
Ahou	*The nofe.*		
Ahow	*Cloth.*		**D**
Aheok	*Lean.*	Dibbe	*A knife.*
Ahoue	*A paddle.*	Dehi	*Large.*
Aite	*Cocoa-nut fkin.*		
Aiper	*No.*		**E**
Amotear	*The cheek.*	Ea	*Yes.*
Anoho	*Sit down.*	Earere	*Black.*
Apeto	*The navel.*	Earrero	*The tongue.*
Arourei	*Hair.*	Eata	*To underftand.*
Ara	*The forehead.*	Enou	*Good for nothing.*
Aree	*A chief.*	Enopo	*Laft night.*
Arere	*Prefently.*	Erepo	*Dirty.*
Ataurremar	*Back of the hand.*	Ete	*Small.*
Alvar	*The back.*	Ettie	*To cry.*
Attah	*Laughing.*	Etar	*The chin.*
Attumata	*Eyebrows.*	Evey	*Frefh water.*
Attoubono	*Shoulders.*		
Aumar	*Breaft.*		**H**
Aupo	*Head.*	Haramy	*Come here.*
Aupee	*A gift.*	Hare	*To go away.*
Awatear	*Elbow.*	Hayar	*A fifh.*

Heis

| Heis | To see. |
| Heaver | Dancing. |

M

Mamai	Sore
Mannue	A bird.
Marhe	Fat.
Mattow	Affronted.
Madure	Apparent.
Mar	To eat.
Manoe	Cocoa-nut oil.
Mayyer	Bananoes.
Mahanner	The sun.
Malomar	The moon.
Martar	Eyes.
Matty	The wind.
Marneoe	Calm.
Maride	Cold.
Mere	To look.
Miou	A nail.
Misou	To starch.
Mity	Good.
Midde	Salt water.
Moerer	A bed.
Momour	The wrist.
Moto	A cut.
Morie	A burning-place.
Moare	A fowl.
Motu	A small island.
Moe	To sleep.
Monour	Deep water.
Moer	An hill.
Muttou	A fish-hook.

N

Nea	Nails.
Nennahi	Yesterday.
Nennahidura	Two days ago.
Nessue	Upper teeth.
Neanear	Singing.

O

Oe	You.
Opu	Belly.
Opey	Rotting or sore.
Otu	Upper lip.
Ouna	By and bye.
Ouar	Rain.
Ouhi	Fire.
Owhy	Stones.
Own	What.
Owrrowrer	Red.

P

Parahi	Stay here.
Papper	A stool.
Pear	A box.
Perrow	To talk.
Pier	A bellyful.
Porode	Hunger.

T

Tarter	Man.
Tasher	That thing.
Taumou	Plated hair.
Taume	A breast-plate.
Tahere	Where

Tanea

Tanear	*Above.*		**W**
Tatare	*White.*	Whatta	*To break*
Teder	*Enough.*	Whoro	*Loſt.*
Teto	*To ſteal.*	Wore	*Yourſelf.*
Terratarne	*A huſband.*	Whoarar	*Well.*
Terrarhanie	*A wife.*		
Tederro	*Below.*		Numbers.
Tiore	*Name.*	1 Atahi.	
Tiporahy	*To ſtrike.*	2 Arour.	
Tio	*A friend.*	3 Torow.	
Topo	*Blood.*	4 Yaw.	
Toupar	*Hips.*	5 Remar.	
Toboi	*Feet.*	6 Vaheine.	
Toa	*An axe.*	7 Hetu.	
Tomallo	*Sweet potatoes.*	8 Wharro.	
Towtow	*Anchor.*	9 Hevar.	
Tourer	*A rope.*	10 Hewrow.	
Toutow	*A ſervant.*	11 Martiti.	
		12 Marrour.	
	U	13 Mortorow.	
Uhiane	*A woman.*	14 Mayyaw.	
Ule	*A bat.*	15 Marremay.	
Ure	*A dog.*	16 Marheine.	
Uru	*Bread-fruit.*	17 Marhetu.	
		18 Marwarru.	
	V	19 Marhevar.	
Varer	*Dreſſed.*	20 Arowratow.	
Vete Vete	*A pearl fiſh-hook.*		
Verride	*Anger.*		
Vennure	*Land.*		
Veſſue	*Place.*		

N. B. The ſame language is ſpoke at the iſlands of Otahitee, Hoahina, Uliateah, Otahaw, Bola Bola, Ohiteroah, and Tabuamana.